Contents

Preface

Every good and excellent thing," wrote Thornton Wilder, "stands moment by moment on the razor edge of danger and must be fought for." He could very well have been writing about public education in the 21st century.

Public education is the vehicle that protects the core values of a democratic society. In the 21st century, leaders of the education enterprise are needed who possess the skills and disposition to *defend the tower*, articulate an educational vision, establish creative problem solving, and foster continuous improvement. Thus, we have written this book, *Qualities for Effective Leadership: School Leaders Speak*.

The individuals who wrote the various chapters are committed to quality leadership of our public schools and university leadership preparation programs. At the same time, the material stresses the importance of dealing with actual problems that confront school leaders. Each author has not only served as a leader of an education system but has also taught either full time or part time at the university level and has conducted workshops and seminars on leadership or written in other publications about the importance of leadership in education.

Chapter 1 is a discussion of the complexities of leadership, issues of the new century that impact on school leaders, and competencies required for successful leadership. The position taken is that of the

French poet Paul Ambroise Valery who once said "the future is not what it used to be." Trends affecting education are discussed and analyzed.

In chapter 2 , the need for strong moral leadership is articulated. Education in the 21st century will require individuals whose leadership acts emanate from knowledge, wisdom, courage, the ability to persuade, and a personal commitment to fairness and justice. Given a choice between being powerful or being good, the author hopes that education leaders will choose to be good.

Chapter 3 deals with the need to create learning communities. Leadership theory is applied to a variety of work conditions. The author presents practical strategies for organizational effectiveness and for establishing community support of public education. Learning communities give direction to education leaders and school systems.

Chapter 4 is a description of how learning communities work. The author stresses the need for entrepreneurial leadership and the obligation for living cooperative leadership patterns. Learning communities are the basis for effective education leadership.

In chapter 5, the leader is portrayed as an anthropologist. The leader of the future is one who understands the context and the culture in which leadership takes place. Leadership acts occur within a specific set of conditions and are strongly influenced by the history and artifacts of the organization. The effective leader appreciates the anthropological necessity to understand when and how to lead education systems.

Chapter 6 identifies the many problems that confront school leaders and articulates what can be done to solve them. Issues presented are those related to demographic changes in student population, the diversity in the nation, and the need for accountability. The emerging requirement is the need to obtain higher results in student academic achievement.

In chapter 7, the case for financial adequacy for public education is argued. The authors examine recent court decisions and establish the basis for providing adequate financial support for all schools, especially those in low wealth school districts, and providing adequacy is the moral obligation of legislators, which many of them have abandoned.

Chapter 8 emphasizes that desire, skill, and ability are insufficient to provide effective leadership in the 21st century. The case is made that exemplary leaders must possess or develop skills in listening, inspiring others, embracing the leader's vision, being forthright when addressing issues, recognizing that the position of power you hold is only temporary, and understanding that you are not the *only fountain of knowledge.* The author provides suggestions for enjoying your achievements and recognizing that paradoxes exist in the leadership role.

In chapter 9, the discussion of leadership and the law reinforces previous chapters that focus on democratic principles, moral and ethical leadership, financial adequacy, and expectations that society has for equity and opportunity. Fundamentally, leaders must recognize and practice those skills necessary to meet legal requirements, at the same time balancing the demands of the various policy bodies that establish the parameters within which an educational system operates.

The concluding chapter 10 is a brief look at what leaders can learn from *great* companies and *high-performing* school districts. The author points out that similar leadership practices are involved in both successful public and private enterprises; and that current and aspiring leaders may want to become familiar with them. In addition, the author suggests that university preparation programs may wish to incorporate some of these findings into their leadership preparation programs.

This book is intended for anyone who has an interest in the effective schooling of our children. It will be of particular interest to school personnel, board of education members, legislators, university professors of leadership, and those involved in developing public policy in education. As W. E. B. DuBois wrote in *Freedom to Learn*, "Of all the civil rights for which the world has struggled and fought for 5,000 years, the right to learn is undoubtedly the most fundamental." Leaders are needed to protect that right. *Qualities for Effective Leadership: School Leaders Speak* also includes an extended index, and the references listed provide additional resources for the study of leadership.

Acknowledgments

This book was inspired by M. Donald Thomas, a colleague and mentor to all of the contributors, including the editor. Don has an undying belief in the principles that serve as the foundation for the public school system in America. He has imbued these principles in his leadership of the school systems he served, the university classes he teaches, the consulting he provides to schools and school districts nationwide, and to each individual he interacts with. The authors of this book have benefited from Don's advice and council at some point in their careers and agreed to participate in this project because of the beliefs they share with Don and each other.

Every project has its ups and downs; this one was no different. I agreed to take on this task two years ago. As with many grand ideas, life's realities intervened and have caused a delay in achieving the dream—a leadership book that would benefit current and future leaders of the education system we all serve. I am deeply indebted to Don and all of the chapter contributors, who have been patient through many delays, for hanging in there and having confidence that the project would come to fruition. As editor, I had the responsibility of putting it all together. Rest assured, I took the assignment seriously. I hope the contributors and those who have heard about the book and have been patiently awaiting its release will forgive the delay.

As is always the case, an editor needs assistance. I would be remiss if I did not recognize my administrative assistant, Vicki Fanning, who on her own time assisted with the editing and preparation of this book. Her expertise, gained through her role as production editor of a professional journal, was invaluable.

Finally, I must express a note of appreciation to my wife, Andrea, who, for 45 years, has been my partner in all of my efforts to write about, present information on, and promote qualities of effective leadership.

Global Perspective on School Leadership

William L. Bainbridge and M. Donald Thomas

The need for educational leaders is urgent and worldwide. This chapter focuses on the important contribution of educational leaders in a global society. Leadership is seen as having a setting, a historical framework, a wholeness of meaning, and a diversity of influences. The authors list five truths of leadership, five reasons why education leadership is more difficult now than ever before, the characteristics that education leaders must possess to be successful, and five imperatives of leadership. Also detailed are the complexities of educational leadership, leadership issues for the 21st century, and necessary leadership qualities.

"A leader is one who, out of madness or goodness, volunteers to take on the woe of a people. There are few so foolish; hence the erratic quality of leadership in the world."

—John Updike

Educational leadership can be madness, or it can make a contribution to improve our schools. It can be a frantic effort to fix everything, or it can be concentrated on a few important items. It can be a futile exercise of power, or it can empower individuals to help themselves. In the face of dramatic social change, a troubled sea of governance conflict, and excessive demands on schools, it can be said that one who aspires to school leadership must be either mad or a supreme egotist. The need for educational leaders is urgent and worldwide; fortunately, there are some who are willing to take on the woe of a people.

COMPLEXITIES OF EDUCATIONAL LEADERSHIP

Educational leadership can be partially understood by a study of leadership literature. Such a study will also help us to understand the complex nature of leadership. The history of educational leadership will never be complete. There will always be a final chapter to be written. Since educational leadership is extremely complex, simple models (events make the person, charisma, a leader for all seasons, the great individual theory, etc.) do not adequately explain the individual or the character of leadership. Leadership must be examined holistically and in context with history. It should not, however, be examined in isolation from the organizations, forces, and events that surround it. Leadership has a setting, a historical framework, a wholeness of meaning, and a diversity of influences.

One theory suggests that social evolution requires three forms of leadership: the formation of ideas, the articulation of those ideas, and, finally, the building of those ideas. The American Revolution saw this triumvirate at work when the ideas formed by John Locke were articulated by the patriots and then built by Benjamin Franklin, George Washington, and Alexander Hamilton. It may be that sounds of violence and radical change are needed before the builders can appear to be moderates. Often, a period of turmoil and conflict is followed by one of cooperation and quiet progress.

There is also a debate as to the merits of shared values between a leader and the group on which the leader aspires to assert influence. Some claim that leadership is possible only when values are similar; others say that leadership cannot occur unless values are divergent. Those who argue for similar values say that leadership is accepted when the leader is trusted and seen as the model for the group. Those who argue for different values say that leadership is the process of changing group values. Their position is that leadership cannot exist without change.

It may be possible that both are needed. The leader must articulate the values of the society but at the same time have some personal values that go beyond those of the group. Leadership is possible only if one has followers. One cannot have followers if the leader's views and values do not coincide with those of the group. But leadership is also the process of going beyond the status quo, exploring new ideas, and creating new forms. In education, leaders must be in tune with the values of their communities if they are to hold their jobs. They must also contribute something from themselves to earn their pay.

Scholars have argued as to whether effective leaders are manipulative or sincere. Some state that the act of leadership is always manipulative, that the leader knows where he or she is going and manipulates others toward those objectives. Others claim that when leaders believe and are committed to their purposes, leadership is sincere. Sincerity is defined as the act of believing one's own propaganda.

There is no perfect model for examining leadership. There are no exact criteria. It may be that leadership is so complex that, at best, we can only obtain clues, study a variety of styles, and partially understand it. We can feel it when it occurs; we know when it is not there.

The complexities of leadership are such that conclusions are dangerous. There is no overwhelming consensus on how leaders become leaders and how they influence the direction of society. There are, however, some things about leadership with which most students of the concept will agree. These *truths* may help us to better understand leadership.

1. Leadership is situational and varies with individuals and events. The situation usually helps make the leader, and at times the leader happens to be in the right place at the right time. Harry Truman is a prime example.

2. There is no single way to prepare leaders or to prepare for leadership. Leaders come from every segment of society and have a variety of styles. There is no set of characteristics which leaders possess, and there is no single educational program which will produce individuals who possess leadership qualities.
3. A leader is someone who has followers. Without followers there is no leadership act. The leader usually helps others attain the goals of the group. The leader guides them to where they wish to go. If no one is going anywhere, there is no need for a leader.
4. Leadership has ethical implications. Even the best intentions may have adverse consequences on others. Sometimes doing what one considers right hurts other people. At the same time, inappropriate leadership acts may have beneficial effects. The leader must always consider the moral validity of what is done or not done. In the behavior of people, the ethical dimensions are always present.
5. The study of historical figures helps us to understand leadership. Socrates teaches us how to make ultimate sacrifices by *taking the hemlock*; Martin Luther King Jr. and Mahatma Gandhi teach us passive moral resistance; and Thomas Jefferson instructs us on the imperatives of education.

LEADERSHIP ISSUES

The issues that face educational leaders are exceedingly complex. Headlines from leadership journals and newsletters portray the breadth and depth of the school leadership challenge. Some include:

- "Take Control Before Negotiations Begin"
- "The Trouble with Standards"
- "How to Lead During Transition"
- "Five Essential Elements of a Team"

- "Make Your People Want to Change"
- "Strong Leaders Delegate"
- "Dealing with Acts of Aggression"
- "Standards are the Life-World of Leadership"
- "The Superintendent as Staff Developer"
- "Strategies for Dealing with High-Stakes State Tests"
- "Predictable Problems in Achieving Large-Scale Change"
- "The Right Questions Lead to the Right Vision"
- "Honesty: The Best Policy for Uncertainty"

Educational leadership is more difficult now than it has ever been. Those who aspire to take on the woe of a people will be confronted with

1. decreasing financial support for public education with increasing support for alternatives to traditional public policy: charter schools, open enrollment vouchers, choice (within and outside of public education), and home schooling (one of the most rapidly developing alternatives to public education).
2. increasing demand for accountability for improving academic quality and extending that quality to an ever-increasing number of children. Educational leaders are to accomplish this with minimal increase in financial support and better utilization of current staffs in order to produce a more highly educated workforce.
3. increasing expectations to better educate children of a pluralistic and troubled society. Educational leaders will be faced with more special education children, more children whose primary language is not English, and a greater number of children who come from nontraditional families. Such an evolution requires a redeployment and expansion of resources to satisfy the demands for accountability.
4. increasing conflict in the governance of education as more and more pluralistic interests are expressed. Conflicts will develop

over the cost of educating special-needs children, appropriate curriculum, safe buildings, choice plans, separation of powers, over-teaching methods, and dozens of other possible conflict areas.

5. pressure to effectively use more and more technology to improve the quality of education. At the same time, the access to and the ability to use technology contributes to greater differences between rich and poor. Technology literacy is also influencing pedagogy and worldwide communications. Given cost, access, and technological literacy issues, however, the majority of schools will play catch-up for decades to come.

NEEDED LEADERSHIP QUALITIES

Faced with these difficult conditions, what do educational leaders of the future need in order to be successful? The qualities needed can be divided into personal competencies and technical competencies. Personal competencies are demanded by the nature of society, and technical competencies are demanded by the nature of the position of educational leadership. A listing of the competencies needed includes:

1. Personal competencies: the ability to
   - listen effectively, understanding both content and feeling;
   - validate the accuracy of information received;
   - speak frankly and clearly, and speak directly to the issue;
   - be positive about life, about self, and about one's work;
   - understand and articulate learning processes;
   - keep current, synthesize knowledge, and utilize research;
   - receive satisfaction and reinforcement from one's work ;
   - self-motivate and inspire colleagues
   - try new ideas, take risks, and encourage others to do so; and

- articulate purpose, establish a vision, and inspire confidence in schools.
2. Technical competencies:
   - Professional and ethical leadership
   - Information management and education
   - Curriculum instruction and learning environment
   - Professional development and human resources
   - Organizational management
   - Interpersonal relationships
   - Financial management and resource allocation
   - Technology and information systems

IMPERATIVES OF LEADERSHIP

Abraham Lincoln was unquestionably one of the great public policy leaders. Writings by and about Lincoln enumerate executive strategies for tough times. In his book, *Lincoln on Leadership,* Donald T. Phillips (1992) details ideas that he suggests Lincoln would embrace today:

- Get out of the office and circulate among your associates.
- Build strong alliances.
- Persuade rather than coerce.
- Subscribe to honesty and integrity as the best policies.
- Never act out of vengeance or spite.
- Have the courage to handle unjust criticism.
- Be decisive.
- Lead by example.
- Be results oriented.
- Choose as your chief subordinates people who crave responsibility and take risks.
- Master the art of public speaking.
- Preach a vision and continually reaffirm it.

Educational leadership in the future will take what Herman Kahn called the quantum leap into a society based on people, not things. Rather than from positions, leadership will emanate from knowledge, from wisdom, from the ability to persuade, and from a personal commitment to fairness and justice. Leadership will be established *through the consent of the governed* and from a basis of ethics, ideas, and persuasion.

The imperatives of this kind of leadership are obvious:

- appreciation and protection of democratic principles;
- protection and extension of basic human rights;
- adherence to ethics, equity, fairness, and justice;
- knowledge of best practices, effective pedagogy, brain development, and other educational research; and
- adherence to the exemplar principle through which outstanding leaders serve as role models to emerging leaders.

Fred M. Hechinger once stated that effective leaders lead by example, by force of ideas, by devotion to fairness and justice. Such are the imperatives of leadership in a time of increasing focus on educational accountability and diversity.

CONCLUSION

Horace Mann (1859) wrote that one should be ashamed to die until he has won some victory for mankind. Henry Kissinger believes that the task of the leader is to get people from vested interest to the public good, from bigotry to tolerance, from hostility to peaceful co-existence.

Leaders in education need to express idealism and practicality. An idealist is one who sees the goal, but who is also willing to provide solutions to the concrete problems that prevent the attainment of the goal. Victory is not achieved by rhetoric. It is achieved by hard work, by support for teachers, by confrontations with hostile forces, and by occasionally facing the possibility of *taking the hemlock*.

Educational leaders have always been positive people—almost missionary in their belief in the perfectibility of the human race. They have never wavered in their strong understanding of the usefulness of schools and education. They have had faith in the purposes of schooling. School leaders have emulated *Pilgrim's Progress* (Bunyan, 1985) in their zeal to provide an effective education for each boy and girl, no matter the obstacles or the difficulties. Their mission has been indestructible, even though many lost their jobs, were stalemated by powerful political forces, or were hampered by the lack of resources.

Being an educational leader is difficult. It is complex. It is rarely honored in song and book. But when the final chapter is written, it will be education and educational leaders who will have contributed most to the protection of democracy, to equity, to justice, and to human dignity. Leaders need to take on the woe of a people, lead by the force of ideas, and govern through the consent of the governed. When they do, they will be honored and respected. They will share in the glory of making a difference and will be praised in the volumes of educational history yet to be written. More important, they will be motivated to attempt even greater accomplishments.

REFERENCES

Bunyan, J. (1985). *Pilgrim's progress*. Chicago: Moody.

Mann, H. (1859). *Challenge to the graduating class of Antioch College*. Yellow Springs, OH: Antioch College.

Phillips, D. T. (1992). *Lincoln on leadership: Executive strategies for tough times*. New York: Warner.

2

Leadership as an Individual: The Hemlock Theory

M. Donald Thomas

This chapter focuses on the moral aspect of leadership. One characteristic that defines great leaders is a passion for a great cause. It incorporates the belief that ordinary people can do extraordinary things. With that belief, the ability to succeed against great odds can be realized. Great leaders are separated from the others because they choose to do what some believe cannot be done. These leaders sometimes must stand up for what is right at great personal risk, even if they must stand alone. The risks are immense, the rewards are few, the work is painful, the critics are legion, but the future is more promising because of what they do.

All leadership behavior is rooted in the soil of morality. Leadership acts are never neutral—they are either *good* or *evil*, as determined by the consequences of what the leader does. Moral leadership requires courage and self-sacrifice. Often it requires that one should *drink the hemlock*. This does not mean that one should always give up his or her life for principle. It does, however, require that leaders sometimes stand up for what is right even when their jobs are in jeopardy.

The great leaders of the world have never had position security: Jesus, Mahatma Gandhi, Socrates, Christopher Columbus, W. E. B. DuBois, Martin Luther King Jr., Thomas Jefferson, Horace Mann. What they did have, however, was personal security. They understood who they were and what needed to be done, even at the risk of their personal safety. The one characteristic that defined each was a passion for a great cause, or *fire in their bellies*. This passion for a great cause can be illustrated by two examples: by a group of individuals who wanted to reform an organization and by a governor who reformed a state's approach to education.

Some 30 years ago, Greg Coffin, Donald Peckenpaugh, and Robert Spillane formed the School Management Study Group (SMSG). Their purpose was to challenge the American Association of School Administrators (AASA). Their cause was to have AASA democratize its governance structure and respond more forcefully to the issues of the day. Coffin's passion was equity for minorities. Peckenpaugh wanted equity for women. Spillane's passion was for handicapped children.

With 20 members and a treasury of $200, they met with AASA leaders and articulated the need for reform within AASA. They had learned well the lesson of history that agencies rarely reform themselves voluntarily. They were so foolish as to threaten a boycott of the national AASA convention. "We will stop the convention dead in its tracks," the three of them confidently stated.

Fortunately for them, and possibly for the convention, Paul Salmon, the executive director of AASA at the time, co-opted SMSG's purposes. He placed most SMSG members on various AASA committees. Salmon responded to SMSG's frustrations, dealt more seriously with the issues, and began a move to democratize AASA governance. The rest is history, not because of the actions of SMSG, but because what Salmon did was right.

Salmon was not in line with the wishes of the AASA board of directors or executive committee. However, he did what he believed was right. Being executive director of AASA was less important to him than responding to the needs of AASA members.

Today, AASA has opened its doors and its windows to minorities, has a more democratic governance structure, and recently served as an exemplar in the treatment of the handicapped. While SMSG exists today as a loosely organized association of educators determined to improve schools, it no longer has the fire in its collective bellies.

As I review the events of that time, I wonder where the passion has gone. Where are the leaders willing to take on the woe of a people? The essential message is that leadership requires a passion for a great cause and the ability to succeed against great odds. If everything were easy, there would be no need for leadership.

Today, it is possible to educate most students better than they have been previously educated. As Ron Edmonds believed, if you have seen one school succeed, how many more do you need to see? Our women, our Native Americans, our Blacks, our Hispanics, our poor, our handicapped, cannot wait forever. The woe of these people calls for dynamic leaders to take it on.

Let me illustrate with one such leader—Richard Riley, former governor of South Carolina and secretary of education of the U.S. Department of Education (1992–2001). Against great odds, he inspired an entire state to improve public education. He convinced South Carolina voters to increase taxes to fund education reform. His "Penny for Education" campaign has now become an exemplar for obtaining public support for schools. His political talents and his ability to persuade others have been adequately reported in the education media, including *The Wall Street Journal, Fortune,* and many other publications.

The real story, however, is one of fire in the belly and taking on the woe of a people. "We have under-educated our people," Riley told me, "and we can't do it any longer. We cannot survive economically, we cannot survive socially without quality education." Riley had a passion for quality education. He was foolish enough to believe that South Carolina children could score in the top quartile on nationally normed tests. He was foolish enough to believe that women could be educated at the same levels as men, and he was foolish enough to believe that most children, regardless of socioeconomic status, could learn the basic curriculum of the school.

As secretary of education, Riley believed, as most great leaders believe, that education is a *noble cause*, and that improving our schools is a moral imperative. What made him a leader is his belief that ordinary people can do extraordinary things. This type of leadership was defined by Andrew S. Grove, former CEO of the Intel Corporation, "Leaders are individuals who make ordinary people do extraordinary things in the face of adversity."

These are the elements of effective moral leadership:

- A passion for a great cause—educating well all of our children
- The ability to inspire ordinary people to do extraordinary things
- The ability to concentrate on what needs to be achieved, not on the obstacles to success
- The ability to know what is the right thing to do

Too many leaders in education worry too much about why we cannot educate well all of our children and not enough about *why* we have not done so. I am still impressed by the comment of a young lady in South Carolina who admonished an education official to stop patting her on the head and concentrate on teaching her children to read. We cannot control the demographic trends in our nation, but we can control how we use our hands.

The Salmon and Riley type of leadership exemplifies the belief in doing the impossible. This type of leadership nurtures and encourages others to work beyond the limits of human endurance. Success is possible despite inadequate financial support, large class sizes, unwarranted state regulation, undermotivated students, and historical neglect. It is a leadership that achieves high performance results regardless of the conditions that one faces.

We must claim, as Thomas Jefferson claimed, that there is a spark of genius in every child, that the perfectibility of man is a basic purpose of public education. It does not matter that *entry-level characteristics* differ. What matters most is that our pedagogy is appropriate for every boy and girl who enters the schoolhouse door.

There are many fine leaders in our schools and in our private sector agencies. What separates the great leaders from the others is the desire to do what some believe cannot be done. If SMSG has taught me anything, it has taught me the lesson and power of passion. Individuals can make a difference. Salmon made AASA a great organization. Riley made South Carolina a better state. If you choose to take on the woe of a people, you, too, can make your school/school district better. If you choose to do so, the risks are immense, the rewards are few, the work is painful, the critics are legion; but the vision is powerful, and our nation is more secure because of what you do.

Each of us should remember the admonition of Julius Adler. At age 102, he regretted the things that he had not done but wished that he had. Leaders who believe in the Hemlock Theory of Leadership will have few regrets.

On January 1, 1863, Abraham Lincoln issued his *Emancipation Proclamation*. Rather than saving the Union, the Civil War became a moral crusade to make men feel free. It was this passion for justice that eventually won the war, even though Lincoln did not live to see the end results.

If there is an emerging pattern of effective leadership, it is one that is based on moral courage. It has been seen in many men and women, such as Anne Hutchinson in the Massachusetts Bay Colony of the 1630s; Rosa Parks; Martin Luther King Jr.; Robert Kennedy; and hundreds of lesser known individuals who every day lead our schools, who, as John Gardner wrote, "believe, with Immanuel Kant, that individuals should be treated as ends in themselves, not as a means to the leader's end, not as objects to be manipulated" (Gardner, 1993, p. 73).

The Hemlock Theory of Leadership does not demand that one *drink the hemlock* as Socrates did. It is, rather, a passion for a great cause, a desire for better schooling for all children. It is leadership that demonstrates courage whenever courage is required in the struggle to provide equal opportunity for each boy and girl, regardless of background, ability, or disability. As Fred Manske Jr. (1999) writes, "Courage is the intangible leadership quality of which greatness is made. It is demonstrated when a person endures severe pressure, conflict, or adversity with grace and dignity. All exceptional leaders seem to have their fair share of it" (p. 81).

This is well illustrated by the reaction of Dr. Martin Luther King Jr. when he received a statement from eight Alabama clergymen. They said,

> However, we are now confronted by a series of demonstrations by some of our Negro citizens, directed and led in the past by outsiders. We recognize the natural impatience of people who feel that their hopes are slow in being realized. But, we are convinced that these demonstrations are unwise and untimely. (Personal communication, April 12, 1963)

Dr. King replied,

> I would not hesitate to say that it is unfortunate that so-called demonstrations are taking place in Birmingham at this time, but I would say in even more emphatic terms that it is even more unfortunate that the white power structure of this city left the Negro community with no other alternative. (Personal communication, April 16, 1963)

The future is not what it used to be. It is one that requires leadership that is grounded in moral principles of justice, courage, and self-sacrifice. There are, unfortunately, too few such leaders. Hence, the necessity for you to become one!

Leaders of the future will possess core values that support public education. These values are so fundamental that one would hold them regardless of position or place of work. As stated by Jim Collins (1999), "Timeless core values should never change; operating practices and cultural norms should never stop changing. A timeless core value in an academic institution, for instance, is freedom of intellectual inquiry."

And finally, leaders of the future will forego power and lead by influence and ideas. Power is like a powerful drink; it can stimulate and motivate, or it can destroy and corrupt. It can make one more sensitive to the need that power should be shared, or it can make one believe that he or she should exercise power on behalf of others. It can be used to support justice or commit evil in the name of *the general good*. No evil, however, can be justified by the use of power for a noble end. Immanuel Kant and his lessons in logic simply will not permit it.

It is my hope that those of us who serve the schools of this nation will use power as little as possible—and that we will understand fully the corrupting nature inherent in the use of power.

REFERENCES

Collins, J. (1999). Aligning action and values. *Leader to leader*. New York: The Drucker Foundation. This article is available on the Leader to Leader Institute Web site, http://leadertoleader.org/leaderbooks/L2L/summer96/collins.html.

Gardner, J. W. (1993). *On leadership*. New York: Free Press.

King, M. L. Jr.(1963). Personal communications, April 12 and 16, 1963.

Manske, F. A., Jr. (1999). Secrets of effective leadership. Memphis, TN: *Leadership Education and Development*, 81

3

Creating Learning Communities in School Systems

Dale L. Brubaker

The following quote aptly summarizes the focus of this chapter: "For the first two-thirds of the twentieth century a powerful tide bore Americans into ever deeper engagement in the life of their communities, but a few decades ago. . . without at first noticing, we have been pulled apart from one another and from our communities" (Putnam, 2000, p. 27).

Robert D. Putnam, the Peter and Isabel Malkin Professor of Public Policy at Harvard University, draws upon vast new data from the *Roper Social and Political Trends* and the *DDB Needham Life Style Surveys* in order to demonstrate how we have become increasingly disconnected from family, friends, neighbors, and social structures. The title of his book, *Bowling Alone: The Collapse and Revival of American Community* (2000), vividly illustrates the present state of our society.

Interestingly, Putnam traces the origin of the key concept, *social capital*, to L. J. Hanifan, state supervisor of rural schools in West Virginia. Hanifan (1920), a practical reformer of the Progressive Era, used social capital to refer to "those tangible substances [that] count for most in the daily lives of people: namely good will, fellowship, sympathy, and social intercourse among the individuals and families who make up a social unit" (p. 130). He added, "The individual is helpless socially, if left to himself" (p. 130).

How does Putnam (2000) explain the collapse of American community? It is not so much that old members have dropped out of community organizations. Rather, it is that community organizations are "no longer continuously revitalized, as they had been in the past, by freshets of new members" (p. 16).

AN AMERICAN DILEMMA

There has always been tension in our society between two forces: collectivism, as represented by community, and individualism. Hedrick Smith (1995) refers to the most dramatic symbol of individualism—the home-run hitter—whose solo performance can "wipe out the opposition with one swift blow" (p. 6). He adds that "it is one of the mindset differences that sets America apart from our greatest economic competitors in the new global game" as "the Germans and Japanese, for example, emphasize teamwork over individual heroics, a more gradual scoring, over the long term rather than the quick, decisive hit" (p. 6).

A visible sign of this dilemma is found in our schools. Teams and teaming are a major part of the rhetoric surrounding our schools—particularly in elementary and middle schools—and yet we continue to give Teacher of the Year Awards. These individual awards are consistent with what Susan Faludi (1999) calls an "ornamental culture . . . constructed around celebrity and image, glamour and entertainment, marketing and consumerism" (p. 35). In short, it is a culture, represented by affiliation such as the NIKE swoosh, "an affiliation grounded in consumption, not production" (p. 83). *Instant affiliation* through consumption crowds out team loyalty and opportunities for true community. Furthermore, collective learning abilities are placed on the back burner as individual showmanship is emphasized.

A conversation with an American teacher or administrator inevitably leads to the matter of parent involvement as a key to creating an effective school. Obstacles to such involvement are many, including overworked parents and family breakdowns. How then can school administrators provide leadership in the renewal of the school as a learning community?

THE RENEWAL OF THE SCHOOL
AS A LEARNING COMMUNITY

A learning organization is "an organization that is continually expanding its capacity to create its own future" (Senge, 1994, p. 14). The first step to be taken is to come together as a faculty and staff to share ideas and feelings associated with being part of learning communities at their best. This positive step invokes a hopeful tone to everything that emerges from this point on in the creation of true community. The following characteristics of true learning communities were identified by educators involved in this activity. "I had a sense of belonging or membership." "We listened to what persons had to say." "We publicly complimented and celebrated persons' talents and contributions." "I felt comfortable whenever we were together." "There was respect for diversity, and we honored different points of view."

The second step is the introduction of a model or map that will give participants a sense of direction in the community-building process. The map will let participants know that the leader is familiar with productive ways to move ahead and is not simply *winging it* or flying the plane while it is being built. At the same time, the leader should make it known that the model or map presented is a starting place or springboard that invites improvement as the learning setting evolves.

M. Scott Peck (1987) has created a promising framework with four stages of community-building: (1) pseudocommunity, (2) chaos, (3) emptiness, and (4) true community.

Pseudocommunity is the stage where leaders try to create instant community by using civilities in order to avoid conflict and individual differences. It is a time when generalizations and platitudes about things held in common prevail. The patter of the cruise ship social director serves as one example. It is the first stage of the accreditation team leader who knows that there is little time to deal with differences and that many tasks must be performed quickly. Reports must be written, and efficiency, rather than effectiveness, is the order of the day. School principals, who feel that parent participation gets in the way of effective teaching and learning, involve parents in school rituals that make them feel good without actually participating in the decision-making life of the school.

Chaos, the second stage, occurs when individual differences emerge. The dissonant voices surface and must be reckoned with by leaders. Peck (1987) believes that "chaos always centers around well-intentioned but misguided attempts to heal and convert" (p. 90). Leaders want things to be *normal* as various constituencies fight to control the agenda. A superintendent of schools entered into a parent-sponsored carnival designed to raise money and create community. He was not bothered when a parent pushed his face into a cream pie for a $25 donation to the school fund, but the principal of the school immediately apologized and closed this booth in an effort to return to normalcy. The sheer noisiness of chaos becomes too much for many leaders who quickly invoke an authoritarian leadership style in order to get things under control.

Emptiness is the third stage of community-making. It is the most difficult stage in creating community and yet is essential as "the bridge between chaos and community" (Peck, 1987, p. 95). When asked what is meant by emptiness, Peck simply says that members of a group "need to empty themselves of barriers to communication" (p. 95). What does Peck mean by barriers to communication? He lists five: (1) expectations and preconceptions; (2) prejudices; (3) ideology, theology, and solutions; (4) the need to heal, convert, fix, or solve; and (5) the need to control.

This stage of community-making was realized during the final class period of the semester in a university seminar. Students were nervous about their papers that were to be handed in that night. Beneath this nervousness was the issue of grades and grading. A 2-hour discussion ensued during which students and their professor emptied themselves of ideas, feelings, and basic assumptions about the reality of the situation. The five barriers to communication listed in the preceding paragraph were overcome by the end of the emotion-filled session. After sharing the expressions of pain, suffering, and brokenness, they all entered a quiet place—the final stage of community-making: true community.

True community is a rare mix of time and place. Once its members achieve this state, they decide where to go from there. Peck (1987) cautions us not to think that life in true community is easier or more comfortable: "But it is certainly more *lively*, more intense. The agony is actually greater, but so is the joy" (p. 105). When you experience true community, you simply know it.

Another model or map for community-building is the Dixon Model for Organizational Learning (Dixon, 1995). This model focuses on the role of information as learning communities are created. Perhaps the most important point Dixon makes is that we must go beyond the simple assumption that organizations should give attention to individual members' learning. She argues that organizations must "establish processes for system-level learning" (p. 1). Her four-step model may be paraphrased as follows: (1) the generation of information as persons act within and outside of the organization, (2) the integration of such information into the organization, (3) the collective interpretation of this information, and (4) action is taken on the basis of the previous three steps. She reminds us that "every step of the cycle must take the collective into account" (p. 1).

It is the matter of collective interpretation that is central to personal and organizational learning. According to Dixon, the following four basic assumptions are central to this matter: (1) all persons must be honestly invited to participate in the generation of information, (2) the egalitarian values of speaking openly without coercion and being respected for this free expression must exist, (3) the size and physical arrangements of the organization must allow for and stimulate interaction between persons and units within the organization, and (4) members of the organization must have and use facilitative processes and skills to participate in discourse.

The skeletal outline of the Dixon model may be useful to the school and school-system leader in creating professional development guidelines that will aid community members in using information in a constructive and creative way. In fact, the Dixon model may be easily translated into a checklist that can be distributed to those interested in creating learning communities.

A third model or map gives special attention to covenants or relationships between and among persons as stages of community-building emerge (Brubaker, 1994, pp. 68–71). Covenants are conditional agreements to do some things and not do others. We enter into covenants with other persons in order to assure predictability in our relationships. The four kinds of covenants in this framework vary as to *intensity* and *duration*.

Covenant 1: *Little intensity and brief duration.* Some meetings and speeches take this form. There is no pretense in many ad hoc situations that community is being created. When such pretense exists, as when the head flight attendant greets you over the public address system or the superintendent of schools calls everyone together at the beginning of the academic year, pseudocommunity exists (Peck, 1987).

Covenant 2: *High intensity and brief duration.* This relationship exists when a police officer gives you a ticket or you are called on the carpet by a bureaucratic superior. The negative spirit of this encounter makes it a perfect fit with top-down bureaucratic organizational structure. A positive spirit exists when an outstanding speaker inspires you during an hour-long presentation. If there is a promise of community by the speaker or host, this is, in effect, pseudocommunity, for the result is short lived.

Covenant 3: *Little intensity but long-term.* The commencement committee in a very tradition-oriented setting serves as an example.

One school system had staff development activities on the third Thursday afternoon of each month. Their ritualistic nature was aptly described by a teacher: "I only hope that I die during an in-service as the distinction between life and death will be so subtle." Any pretense that these activities are community building, would immediately make it clear that this was a pseudocommunity.

Covenant 4: *Intense and long term.* This is the rarest kind of covenant because of the human and nonhuman resources demanded. Ownership by parties to the covenant is obvious in the seriousness and humor exhibited by persons who enter into true community. Persons of opposing views share a mutuality of mission in spite of their differences, and they care enough about each other and the community to truly listen to each other. Many and diverse talents are publicly identified and honored.

It has been demonstrated that models such as those presented here can provide educational leaders with a map of the territory known as community-building. These models or maps provide leaders and community members with context for particular decisions and events.

SUMMARY AND CONCLUSION

Educational leaders in the 21st century are challenged by the fact that many persons, young and old, feel disconnected from family, friends, neighbors, and social structures. The collapse of American community begs for revival of community in general, and learning communities in particular. Brokenness of community is compounded by an American dilemma or contradiction: the forces of community and individualism are often at odds with each other.

School and school-system leaders are in a position to make a difference in community-making. The leader's passion for this endeavor sets the tone after which mechanisms must be in place to realize his or her vision for creating true community. The first step is to have those interested in community-building share their experiences as part of learning communities at their best. The positive nature of this enterprise is complemented by a profile of those feelings and ideas associated with being part of a true learning community. The second step is to have models or maps that can be shared with others interested in community-making. Three maps were presented in this chapter, each serving as a guide for action and assessment of progress.

A major benefit in giving leadership to the creation of learning communities is that leaders are so focused on collective and personal learning that ego-related problems will be minimized, and the twin pitfalls of boredom and depression will simply not exist.

REFERENCES

Brubaker, D. L. (1994). *Creative curriculum leadership.* Thousand Oaks, CA: Corwin.

Dixon, N. (1995). A *practical mode for organizational learning.* Greensboro, NC: Center for Creative Leadership, Issues and Observations.

Faludi, S. (1999). *Stiffed.* New York: Morrow.

Hanifan, L. J. (1920). *The community center.* Boston: Silver Burdett.

Peck, M. S. (1987). *The different drum.* New York: Simon and Schuster.

Putnam, R. D. (2000). *Bowling alone: The collapse and revival of American community.* New York: Simon and Schuster.

Senge, P. M. (1994). *The fifth discipline: The art and practice of the learning organization.* New York: Doubleday.

Smith, H. (1995). *Rethinking America.* New York: Random House.

Entrepreneurial Leadership:
Learning Communities at Work

Donald C. Lueder

In this chapter, "entrepreneurial leadership" and the conceptual framework on which it is based are discussed. The conceptual framework guides entrepreneurial leaders as they work with teachers, students, and parents to design a "community of learners." The framework includes a description of the philosophy, nature, and character of a learning community. Entrepreneurial leadership is not a "silver bullet" or "cookbook" of procedures to tell the leaders what to do. Rather, it is a foundation for leaders to follow as they work to develop themselves and others to be creative learners within a community of learners.

In considering the discussion of a learning community that follows, most people would probably perceive this type of organization favorably and would look forward to working in such an environment. However, if this is true, why is it that most schools are not *learning communities*? Senge, Kleiner, Roberts, Ross, and Smith (1994) argue—and I agree—that one reason people have not created such organizations is the lack of appropriate leadership. They say, "People have no real comprehension of the type of commitment it requires to build such an organization. Learning organizations demand a new view of leadership." The traditional view of leaders is that of exceptional individuals who implement their visions, set directions, make key decisions, and motivate the followers. This perception evolves from an individualistic (great person) and *non-systemic* model of leadership. It is the *John Wayne* approach to leadership, a *saddle up and take charge* strategy. Creating a learning community, however, requires a more subtle and comprehensive leadership approach. The leader's goal is to help build an organization where "people continually expand their capacity to understand complexity, clarify vision, and improve shared mental models" (Senge, 1990, p. 340). This is not an easy task, and it requires *entrepreneurial* skills to build such organizations. The entrepreneurial leader takes on the task of designing, organizing, developing, and managing an enterprise or organization—in this case a learning community. He or she is an individual who can plan for the future and can adapt to the challenges of a changing society, changing values, and changing demographics.

While the typical entrepreneur is usually in the business of making a monetary profit, the person leading a community of learners is in the business of developing people. The educational entrepreneurial leader's goal is to increase the social and academic development of the children and the other stakeholders as well. The entrepreneurial leader is ahead of the pack in his or her thinking and view of the world. He or she will be the *Bill Gates* of the education world, anticipating the future trends and responding to needs of the children, parents, and community.

The entrepreneurial leader is an agent of change and must provide vision and meaning to the organization as he or she helps to create a learning community. DePree (1997) draws a distinction between vision and sight: "We can teach ourselves to see things the way they are. Only with vision can we begin to see things the way they can be" (pp. 116–117). DePree is describing the future-focused quality of entrepreneurial leadership that is essential in creating learning communities.

Future-focused leadership is the ability to look beyond the present circumstances and envision an image of the future that recognizes and responds to the need for change. A community of learners that has a future-focused culture will deal with what is possible and what new opportunities are available and will not dwell on what is wrong and what needs to be fixed.

Creating this type of environment is an awesome task, and entrepreneurial leaders will need a *map* to guide them along the path to a learning community. The purpose of this chapter is to provide such a map.

WHERE TO START?

"Would you tell me please, which way I ought to go from here?" asked Alice to the Cheshire Cat. "That depends a good deal on where you want to get to," said the Cat (Carroll, 1946, p. 41). Like, Alice, as we begin our journey to create a learning community, it is critical that we know where we want to go and why before we plan how to get there. Once the destination is determined, not only do we want to reach our goal but also we want to get there in the most effective and efficient manner. Therefore, to be most successful, the creation of a learning community requires a well-thought-out plan based on a strong conceptual framework.

While the entrepreneurial leader needs to operate from a well-developed plan, he or she must, at the same time, remain flexible. As the learning community is being formed, the school is functioning, and family and community life are ongoing. It is the proverbial case of *building the airplane as you are flying it*. As the entrepreneurial leader attempts to make significant changes, many variables will be continually changing and evolving. However, there is nothing more constant than change. Therefore, entrepreneurial leaders have to be able to adjust, modify, and adapt to the changing conditions.

The experience of the planning process itself helps to develop commitment among the various stakeholders. As Deal and Peterson (1994) note,

Good planning serves as a meaningful ritual that draws people together emotionally and spiritually. Values and hopes are connected to objectives. The planning ritual provides the opportunity to break down the isolation and individualism of teaching through collaborative discussion, collegial sharing, and reflection practice. All can be powerful cultural experiences. (p. 101)

Consequently, as a plan is designed, the process should include the perceptions and judgments of the major stakeholders: the school's faculty and staff, parents, and members of the community. As we shall see, this concept of shared decision-making is fundamental in a learning community. When entrepreneurial leaders are attempting to create a community of learners, they are in the business of restructuring the way the students, faculty, and parents work together. Changing the way people work together involves the development of new roles and relationships. For this to happen, usually a paradigm shift must occur. Giving up a way of thinking is not easy for most people, and helping them to accept a different *reality* is a major challenge for the entrepreneurial leader.

The entrepreneurial leader, therefore, must be able to *see the big picture* and match his or her vision of learning, schooling, organizations, and human processes to the conceptual framework. Consequently, understanding the various concepts, processes, and structures underlying a learning community is an essential step for the entrepreneurial leader. This understanding contributes to the entrepreneurial leader's mental model of learning communities.

The strategies that the entrepreneurial leader uses to help create a learning community will be based on his or her mental model of the structures and processes involved. This is crucial because the creation of a learning community is as much a process as it is a structure.

Senge et al. (1994) define "mental models" as "deeply ingrained assumptions, generalizations, or even pictures or images that influence how we understand the world and how we take action" (p. 8). The mental models are influenced greatly by the leader's values, beliefs, experiences, and background. This is why an entrepreneurial leader must be aware and conscious of his or her mental model of a learning community before he or she begins the journey to create such an entity.

MEMORABLE EDUCATIONAL EXPERIENCES

Our mental models about education are greatly affected by our educational experiences as we grow up. Let's think about some of these experiences. Think back and recall one or two of your most memorable educational experiences. Did they occur in or out of the classroom? Did they occur in or out of the school environment? Did they occur during the regular school day or after? When I asked groups of graduate students, teachers, and administrators to describe their most memorable educational experiences, their responses were varied, interesting, and revealing. For example, one college dean related how his fourth-grade teacher used to take him and his classmates out into the desert in his big red truck. On those days, they would experience the environment together: looking at things, talking together, reflecting on what they saw and felt, and eating good food.

In another case, a graduate student related how her grandmother instilled in her a love for the study of science. Her grandmother was an amateur naturalist, and she would take her on walks in the woods and fields. Together they explored and studied the wonderful world of plants, animals, and rocks.

An associate superintendent recalled that her most memorable educational experience occurred when her high school band director asked her to conduct the band for the day. She was the drum major, and the band was preparing for a big marching competition. They had been practicing throughout the summer. She was excited and honored to be chosen to lead the band, especially since the competition was scheduled for the next day. This recognition was very important to her.

One man told about his magnificent high school language arts teacher who made the lessons on Shakespeare come *alive* for him. The teacher would sing songs and read poetry related to the Shakespearean period. She would have the class study and act out parts from the various plays. At the end of the year, the class would make a presentation to the whole school, and he had a major role in one of the productions.

One thing that the experiences appear to have in common is the conditions of the environment in which they occurred. They happened in energizing situations where the individuals were totally involved and committed. They were memorable because the experiences helped to develop the participants' innate capacities for learning, and the outcomes of the experiences contributed significantly to the learner's overall social and academic development. The academic development would be what Schlechty (1997) calls "knowledgeable work." These are outcomes that involve "transforming information into usable propositions, organizing information in ways that inform decisions and actions, producing products that require others to apply or use information, or arranging and rearranging concepts and ideas in useful ways" (p. 46).

The social dimension of the outcomes of the memorable educational experiences is equally important. This aspect involves the development of the individual's capacity to be sensitive, inquisitive, engaging, caring, and a motivated learner. The two dimensions, of course, are closely related and build upon one another.

Another commonality is that there was always a *significant* person who helped create the learning situation or environment, which was inspiring, nurturing, engaging, and fulfilling. Sometimes the person who provided the experience was a former teacher and other times it was a parent, relative, or other special individual. I would argue that these experiences transpired in situations and environments that we will be referring to as *learning communities.* These are conditions where everyone is learning and growing together, and the focus is on both the social and academic development. In each case, someone was instrumental in creating the learning community.

· A CONCERN

I do find it somewhat disconcerting, however, that so many of the memorable experiences that were recalled happened outside the formal classroom and often away from the school. Certainly, I would not expect that all memorable educational experiences would occur in formal educational settings. However, I would hope and expect that classrooms and schools would be places where memorable educational experiences were more common. I am afraid if we were asked to relate some of our less positive educational experiences, the settings for many of the stories would be former classrooms.

This assumption is supported by the high number of students who physically or psychologically *drop out* of school each year. My guess is that we would gather some sobering evidence if we were to ask the school dropouts about their most memorable educational experiences, not many would be *in-school* stories. When I asked individuals who left school without graduating to tell me why they left, the answers usually centered on two reasons: *the classes were boring,* and *nobody cared.*

I believe one of our challenges as educational leaders is to help create environments that support, promote, and enhance learning for all: students, teachers, administrators, and parents. These environments should be designed to engage all of the participants to become lifelong learners. Kleine-Kracht (1993) states:

> We can no longer afford to conceive of schools simply as knowledge distribution centers. The school must be much more than a place of instruction; it must also be a center of inquiry, that is a producer as well as a transmitter of knowledge. A school organized as a center of inquiry is an institution characterized by a pervasive search for meaning and rationality in its work.

WHAT IS THE PURPOSE OF SCHOOLING?

A concept that contributes to the vision of a learning community is our notion about the purpose of schooling. Scholars have debated this question for centuries, and many credible arguments have been made to support many diverse opinions. However, I would like to offer a basic definition. I propose that the fundamental purpose of schooling is to increase the social and academic development of the children. However simplistic this view might be, I believe that all of the various programs, activities, and events in schools should be focused on this purpose.

Consequently, all programs, activities, and events should be considered to be aspects of the overall curriculum. Therefore, the term *extracurricular* as it relates to programs and activities is misleading. Music, athletics, club activities, and theatre programs are very much part of the curriculum because they should be increasing the social and academic development of the children. I recognize that this is not always the case, but I believe a learning community would not have these inconsistencies.

THE CURRICULUM

To better understand the process of schooling, it is helpful to think about the curriculum as two separate and interrelated components: the *outer curriculum* and the *inner curriculum*. Brubaker (1994) says that the outer curriculum is the formal course of study, encompassing the syllabi, benchmarks, standards, texts, pacing guides, and so forth. The outer curriculum should be a well-conceived educational plan that is appropriate for all students. The inner curriculum, on the other hand, includes the processes, procedures, and environments in which the outer curriculum is delivered. The inner curriculum evolves from the beliefs, values, and assumptions (mental models) about education held by those implementing the outer curriculum. As we shall see, these processes, especially the inner curriculum processes, are closely related to mental models and the nature of a learning community.

I believe the following two concepts will help us to understand the nature of learning communities. First, the purpose of schooling is to increase the social and academic development of the children, and second, the curriculum is both the structured course of study and the processes of delivering and implementing the course of study.

DEFINITIONS OF LEARNING COMMUNITIES

Many authors have attempted to describe their mental models of a learning community to others. Roland Barth (1990) states that, "A community of learners is a place where students and adults alike are engaged as active learners in matters of special importance to them, and where everyone is thereby encouraging everyone else's learning." Another definition is "a community of colleagues gathered to study and advance knowledge. Some of our colleagues are children, who although our clients, are collaborators in learning" (Joyce, Wolf, and Calhoun 1993, p. 8). Many years ago, Schaefer (1967) argued that learning communities "are places where both teachers and students are learners, and where learning is an active process that takes place in many different ways."

In Senge's 1990 work, *The Fifth Discipline: The Art and Practice of the Learning Organization,* he describes his mental model of a learning community. He views a learning organization as a place where people continually expand their capacity to create the results they truly desire, where new and expansive patterns of thinking are nurtured, where collective aspiration is set free, and where people are continually learning how to learn together. He believes "a learning organization is a place where people are continually discovering how they create their reality, and how they can change it" (p. 13).

Hill, Pettit, and Dawson (1995) argue that,

At the heart of the concept of the school as a learning community lies a total commitment of the value of learning for all members. This commitment is underpinned by beliefs that learning is inherently enjoyable and exhilarating, that all members have the capacity to learn, and that each person brings to the organization unique abilities which must be acknowledged and utilized. (p. 2)

The notion of lifelong learning is a philosophical driving force within a learning community where learning focuses on process as well as content and product. Cooper and Boyd (2000) maintain that a collaborative learning community is "a philosophy as well as a place; it is a way of being as well as a working model. It is a mindset as well as a map." With learning as the focus, collaborative learning communities "help students learn the attitudes, knowledge and skills that benefit all in the community, and community members become partners in facilitating and expanding the learning process" (p. 1).

Brown and Moffett (1999) present a discussion of a "heroic" school. I believe what they call a heroic school would be considered a learning community. They describe a heroic school as an inclusive community of lifelong learners characterized by academic rigor, professional excellence, and extraordinary caring for the welfare of each child it serves. I would add, and I think they would too, that the caring and nurturing should be extended to everyone in the community, including the parents.

A WARNING

Rebecca van der Bogert (1998) warns us that,

The term *community of learners* is currently about as common and revered as motherhood and apple pie. Bringing the concept to reality is far more difficult than baking an apple pie [although] the need for ongoing nurturing and the degree of challenge are perhaps comparable to motherhood. (p. 71)

Cooper and Boyd (2000) express a concern that "With all the buzzwords and fads in education, 'collaborative learning community' has the potential to lose its meaning, or lose its potency" (p. 1).

These are legitimate concerns. New programs are implemented all the time, and many quickly fade away or remain dormant. Someone once said that educational programs are like cemeteries, *you keeping adding to the total, but you never take any away.* Dale Brubaker (1994) addresses this issue when he writes about new educational programs being viewed as the *flavor of the month*. This is a danger related to the notion of learning communities. These are important concerns. For those who wish to implement and develop learning communities in their organizations, it is vital that they understand the underlying principles of a learning community and determine if they fit their mental models of such organizations.

CLASSICAL FOUNDATION

The philosophy of learning communities has its *roots* in classical motivational, psychological, and organizational theory. The conceptual framework for learning communities can be traced back to works of such scholars as Abraham Maslow, Douglas McGregor, Rensis Likert, Chris Argyris, Jacob Getzels, and Egon Guba. For example, in Maslow's (1965) treatise on Eupsychian management, he lists some assumptions that would be fundamental to designing a learning community. His assumptions included such things as the following:

- Everyone is to be trusted.
- Everyone is to be informed as completely as possible of as many facts and truths as possible.
- There is no dominance-subordination hierarchy in the jungle sense or authoritarian sense.
- Everyone will have the same ultimate managerial objectives and will identify with them no matter where they are in the organization.
- There is good will among all the members of the organization rather than rivalry or jealousy.

- Everyone can enjoy good teamwork, friendship, good group spirit, good group harmony, good belongingness, and group love.
- Everyone prefers to feel important, needed, useful, successful, proud, respected.
- A tendency to improve things . . . to put things right, make things better, to do things better.

Also, the Theory Z assumptions presented by McGregor (1960), about regard for people, participation, and expectations, also adhere to those who would be found in a learning community. A leader ascribing to Theory Z assumptions would expect the participants in a learning community to be motivated to seek responsibility, to make good decisions, and to view learning as natural and as play. Chris Argyris (1971) argued that Theory Z assumptions would give rise to behavioral patterns wherein an educational leader would seek to create an environment where students and teachers would use their talents to reach shared goals through participative decision-making, open communications, and self-direction, and -control.

Likert (1961), discussing management patterns, describes four different organizational types ranging from a "closed" System 1 (Exploitive-Authoritative) to an "open" System 4 (Participative) characterized by widely dispersed decision making, open communication, friendly interaction, and a high degree of confidence and trust. A learning community could be described as a System 4. Finally, when Getzels and Guba (1957) describe organizations as systems, they identify three major sets of roles that individuals play, roles that address the institution expectations, group intentions, and individual needs. Basically, this model postulates that the interaction of organizational roles, individual self-interests, and the group intentions would determine the levels of job satisfaction and conflict.

As would be expected, the research shows that there is greater satisfaction and less conflict among organization members if the social system—the school in this case—supports and aligns all three sets of roles. These concepts are important because together they help describe the organization's unique climate (personality, tone, or ethos).

These examples illustrate that the philosophy of learning communities is not new. The conceptual framework of a learning community has evolved from these classical works, as have the following concepts.

ORGANIZATIONAL CLIMATE

As noted, the interaction of organizational roles, individual self-interests, and the group intentions blend to develop an organization's unique climate (personality, tone, or ethos). Owens (2001) refers to organizational climate as "the study of perceptions that individuals have of various aspects of the environment in the organization." Organizational climate, therefore, is an abstract concept of the attributes of leadership and group behavior operating within an organization. For example, the elements of Likert's (1961) management styles would help describe an organization's climate.

If organizational climate is basically how the organization is perceived, then we must keep in mind that all perceptions are *real* to the beholders, whether they are accurate or inaccurate. Therefore, the perceptions held by the organization's members about the climate will have an effect on the behavior and interactions of the individuals within the organizations, such as students, teachers, parents, and administrators.

ORGANIZATIONAL CULTURE

The notion of *organizational culture* is an extension of the concept of organizational climate. Organizational culture refers to the values, beliefs, norms, traditions, rituals, and assumptions that are common in the organization. Schein (1985, as cited in Owens, 2001) defines organizational culture as "the body of solutions to external and in-ternal problems that has worked consistently for a group and that is therefore taught to new members as the correct way to perceive, think about, and feel in relation to those problems." Deal and Kennedy (1982) further define organizational culture in more prac-tical terms. They describe shared values as "what is important," be-liefs as "what we think is true," and behavioral norms or culture as "how we do things around here." Put another way, a learning com-munity's culture is the *glue* that holds the organization together and helps set the direction of the organization.

The notion of organizational culture is a useful concept because many of the characteristics of processes operating within a learning community are in essence the descriptors of an organizational cul-ture. This concept of culture supports the notion that a community of learners is the product of the interaction of process and structure. Owens (2001) reports that it is widely accepted that changing an or-ganization's culture is one of the most critical factors in improving the performance of schools. He paraphrases Kilmann, Saxton, and Serpa (1985) and argues,

> The culture of the educational organization shapes and molds as-sumptions and perceptions that are basic to understanding what it means to be a teacher. The culture informs the teachers as to what it means to teach, what teaching methods are available and approved for use, what pupils or students are like—what is possible and what is not. The culture also plays a large role in defining for teachers their com-mitment to the task; it evokes the energy of the teachers to perform the task, loyalty, and commitment to the organization and its ideals.

Consequently, it is essential that the entrepreneurial leader be knowledgeable of the organization's culture and not lose sight of the fact that any effective change in culture must evolve from the exist-ing culture. He or she must recognize the existing culture and build upon it, not attempt to institute a totally new culture. Any attempt to do this will likely generate feelings of resentment, anger, and resistance and result in creating a *toxic culture* rather than a positive one. No one likes to feel that they are being *fixed*. Rather, the entrepreneurial leader will work, using shared decision making, to build a learning community on the strengths of the existing culture. Imposing your *culture* on an organization goes against a basic premise of a learning community: shared decision-making.

PROCESSES

A learning community is a system comprised of many interrelated processes or components. These processes evolve from the basic premise of the community: shared decision-making. Cooper and Boyd (2000) list the organizational processes that are characteristic of a learning community:

- Shared vision and outcomes for students.
- An open, trusting, caring culture that is manifested through stories, rituals, and traditions as well as futuristic thinking and consistent community-building.
- Procedures for acknowledging participation and contribution of members.
- Supportive structures and policies to implement the vision and facilitate change.
- A flexible design for change and for implementing research-based innovations.
- Procedures for continual assessment and evaluation for school successes and failures.
- Opportunities for sustained professional development and collaborative reflective practices.
- Assessment procedures that continuously measure students' ability to use knowledge in a variety of contexts, using a variety of assessment methods and a variety of assessors, including student self-assessment.

- Practices in classrooms and throughout the school community that are aligned to a core philosophy and to the principles of living systems. (p. 5)

Senge et al. (1994) also present a list of conditions they feel would characterize a learning organization:

- People feel they are doing something that matters to them personally and to the larger world.
- Every individual in the organization is somehow stretching, growing, or enhancing his/her capacity to create.
- People are more intelligent together than they are apart.
- Visions of the direction of the enterprise emerge from all levels. The responsibility of top management is to manage the process whereby new emerging visions become shared visions.
- People feel free to inquire about each other's (and their own) assumptions and biases. There are few (if any) sacred cows or undisputable subjects.
- People treat each other as colleagues. There's a mutual respect and trust in the way they talk to each other and work together, no matter what their positions may be.
- People feel free to try experiments, take risks, and openly assess the results. No one is *killed* for making a mistake. (p. 51)

It is noteworthy that most of these processes and conditions can be traced back to the classical works described earlier. These characteristics represent the various authors' mental models of a learning community. I believe these lists of processes are useful because they describe the character and nature of a learning community.

A SYSTEM APPROACH

While each process is important in itself, the processes and conditions should be perceived as integral aspects of a vital thriving system. Each item is interrelated with the other. For example, you wouldn't expect to have open, honest two-way communications if there was not a high level of trust and regard between the communicators.

This idea of a learning community being a system is crucial to this discussion if we accept the notion that a learning community is as much process as product. The assumption is that the processes and structures come together to act as a system to expand the capacities of its members. Fundamental to the system approach is the concept that one component cannot be changed without affecting other components. Therefore, being a system, a learning community loses some of its direction if the leader concentrates on a particular aspect, or process, without considering the effect on the whole. As Senge et al. (1994) point out, "If you cut a cow in half, you would not have two small cows" (p. 25). All the processes work together to produce the desired effects.

A *stable* organizational system is in a dynamic state of equilibrium called *homeostasis*: operating but not changing its system. A metaphor for a stable system would be a cork floating down a stream. The cork is moving with the flow of the current, but it is neither sinking nor rising in the water. It is *stable*. Therefore, to change an organization, the system would be taken out of homeostasis to produce *disequilibrium*. After an intervention is implemented and the organization has moved to the desired state, the organization will seek to restore its equilibrium. This type of systemic change is involved when creating a learning community.

During this process of change, if the members of the community are acting together they are likely to produce greater organizational energy. This phenomenon of the components of a system interacting as a whole to create *energy* is known as *synergy*. Synergy is a physical science term that means the sum of the parts is greater than the whole.

The idea is that the total effect of the different community members (students, teachers, administrators, and parents) is much more than the total of them acting separately. This is a desired effect in a learning community. Consequently, the leader must be mindful of the systemic nature of organizations. As stated above, the entrepreneurial leader must be able to understand the big picture before he or she can understand the little pictures.

THE ENTREPRENEURIAL LEADER AS TEACHER

For the entrepreneurial leader to create a learning community, he or she assumes many roles, but none is more important than that of a teacher. The leader as teacher is an encompassing role that supercedes and combines many other roles, such as designer, steward, and evangelist. Entrepreneurial leaders as teachers must play all of these roles as they help with the design, nurture the process, and inspire the members. I use the term *teacher* interchangeably with *coach*. In a community of learners, the leader should be *a guide from the side, not a sage from the stage*. It is the role of the entrepreneurial leader to facilitate, not to dictate.

Using this approach is critical in helping to develop a learning community. Senge (1990) reports that when teams seek to develop their learning capacities, frustrations occur when they

(1) lack the power to act in the domain about which they are learning, (2) lack the organizational support to sustain sufficient time and energy to develop new learning, or (3) lack a deep commitment to do the hard work required of them personally and interpersonally. (p. xvii)

It is imperative, therefore, that the entrepreneurial leader share or delegate this power, provide the support, and help to develop the team members' mental models of the mission, philosophy, and structure and the processes underlying a learning community.

For example, in the preceding discussion, I have presented some aspects of my mental model of a learning community and the conceptual framework on which it is based. The model is founded on my values, beliefs, experiences, and background and is linked with various theories and concepts. My vision of the structures and processes within a learning community are aligned with the mental model. However, while my mental model is important to me, it is only my view. In a learning community, the goal is for the participants to operate from a *shared mental model*. The shared model drives the learning community. This concept is an integral and fundamental aspect of a learning community.

Consequently, in the role of teacher, I must identify and affirm my mental model before attempting to build a learning community. Then, in turn, with my help, the other members of the potential community would also identify and confirm their models. Using the philosophy underlying a learning community, the entrepreneurial leader will use coaching strategies to successfully interface his or her mental model with the mental models of the various shareholders to create a *shared model* of a learning community.

This is why the entrepreneurial leader must have a strong sense of self. John Heider (1985) says that effective leaders know where they stand and know what they stand for. He argues that it is impossible to lead others into meaningful conversations about deeply held beliefs, about relationships, and about learning without self-understanding.

The entrepreneurial leader as teacher will attempt to communicate his or her mental model and vision, while actively listening to understand the members' models and visions. Kofman and Senge (1993) state that learning communities provide

> spaces for generative conversations and concerted action (where) people can talk from their hearts and connect with one another in the spirit of dialogue. Their dialogue weaves a common ongoing fabric and connects them at the deep level of being. When people talk and listen to each other this way, they create a field of alignment that produces tremendous power to invent new realities in conversation and bring about these new realities in action. (p. 16)

An Indian proverb says that one *learns more with the ear than with the tongue.*

While identifying and affirming a shared model of a learning community is crucial for the entrepreneurial leader, each member of the community is encouraged to support a model that ascribes to his or her sense of ethics, morality, equity, equality, and principle. A person needs to be true to himself or herself.

At the same time, however, the members should be willing to change, modify, and enhance their model or paradigm. As stated previously, one of the tasks of the entrepreneurial leader is to effectively manage change, and this is an aspect of productive change. Remember that nothing is more solid than change as you attempt to create a community of learners.

The entrepreneurial leader as teacher must help and inspire the members to be active partners in the learning community. These are partnerships comprised of all of the stakeholders: students, parents, faculty, staff, and administrators. The partnerships are collaborative relationships designed primarily to produce positive educational and social effects with children while being mutually beneficial to all other parties involved.

The collaborative relationships in a learning community are formed on the assumption that learning is a shared responsibility and that all partners are *equal* players. Equal, in this case, means that each member of the community contributes in major ways to the success of others and that everyone has a stake in determining the path to the common goal of learning. It is recognized that each student, teacher, parent, and staff member possesses unique strengths, resources, and expertise that can have a positive impact on the learning process.

As DePree (1997) notes, these organizations should provide "nourishment" for all its members. He writes, "The nourishment of individuals lies at the heart of vital organizations, and the nourishment of individuals begins with the opportunity to learn" (p. 105). Cooper and Boyd (2000) support the notion that collaboration is the foundation of a learning community. Their view is that in a community of learners the participants work together for common goals, sharing leadership and power and appreciating and celebrating diversity.

THE POLITICS OF PARTNERSHIPS

Laswell (1936) defined politics in the title of his book as: *Who Gets What, When, and How*. This is a good straightforward definition and fits the political context of a partnership. I contend that we are all motivated by self-interests to get what we want. If the term *self-interests* seems a bit harsh, then the word *needs* can be used. However, I maintain that the act of influencing others to meet our self-interests is what the political process is about. While this may sound manipulative, meeting our self-interests by influencing others is not inherently a positive or a negative act. For example, if you have a good relationship with your significant other, then each of you is meeting some of your self-interests through the relationship. When this is occurring, you would say that you have an enduring partnership, and the partnership will last as long as both of you continue to feel that some of your individual self-interests are being met.

With the present definition of partnerships, the phrase, *to produce a positive educational and social effect with children, while being mutually beneficial to all other parties involved*, relates to the political process. While the child's self-interests are the main focus of the partnership, the other parties are also wanting to have some of their self-interests or needs satisfied. For the partnership to be effective and long-lasting, the relationship must meet some of the needs of the parents, teachers, principals, and community members as well as those of the children.

We may initially be able to get educators, community leaders, and family members excited about entering into a partnership to create a learning community, but it will be hard, if not impossible, to keep them actively involved and committed if they do not see some direct payoff for themselves. In a partnership, the self-interests of all of the stakeholders have to be addressed in order for the relationship to work. If the children's needs are met but not the self-interests of the other parties, the partnership will suffer.

Therefore, knowing and understanding the political process is important in planning, implementing, and maintaining a learning community. It is essential that the entrepreneurial leader identify the self-interests of all the parties: the child, families, and school. He or she needs to ask: *What are the things, in addition to the concern for the children, that will influence the different parties to be active partners?* Determining what the different stakeholders want and need will help us decide what strategies to use to create and build the partnerships. The entrepreneurial leader as teacher then *coaches* the members to help them meet their self-interests while building the community.

SUMMARY

Learning communities should not be seen as ends in themselves but, rather, as a means for students, teachers, and families to work together to enhance the academic and social growth of children. Creating a community of learners is more of a process—based on a collaborative and helping attitude and belief system—than a product. Learning communities are environments in which people help each other so that they can help the children. Uhl and Perez-Sehls (1995) contend that the collaborating staff relishes opportunities to share ideas about teaching. These collaborators value and appreciate the collegial interdependencies in ways that reach deep into the heart of their schools and classrooms, and they perceive individual and group risk-taking as learning opportunities.

Sergiovanni (1996) also argues that participation in a community of learners has a powerful effect on like-minded colleagues. The collaborative relationships help them to increase their knowledge and skills in the classroom and to adapt their teaching strategies to more effectively meet student needs. Where such collegiality is high, teachers have more positive views of teaching and teach more successfully.

Learning communities offer the parties the opportunity to effectively perform their individual roles and fulfill their responsibilities while meeting their needs. These communities are organizations where the members can identify and concentrate on the sources of the educational and social problems rather than on the symptoms. Problems such as low achievement, poor attendance, dropouts, misbehavior, teenage pregnancy, and drug abuse are symptoms of more deeply rooted social and family issues like poverty, dysfunctional family relationships, lack of health care, and poor parenting skills and knowledge. I believe that most social problems will ultimately be solved through education. Therefore, it is imperative that we work together on doing the right things in the right way. It is unlikely that these social and family problems will be solved unless we do. Michael Fullan (1993) states,

> The future of the world is a learning future. . . . It is a world where we will need generative concepts and capacities. What will be needed is the individual as inquirer and learner, mastery and know-how as prime strategies . . . teamwork and shared purpose which accepts both individualism and collectivism as essential to organizational learning. (pp. vii–viii)

Creating learning communities appears to be a viable strategy to help reach this goal. Being part of a learning community will enable administrators, teachers, parents, and community members to come together as partners to deal with education issues. It is the task of the entrepreneurial leader to help the members of the learning community understand the *big picture*, decide where they *want to go and why*, and then collaboratively develop a plan on how to get there.

REFERENCES

Argyris, C. (1971). *Management and organizational development.* New York: McGraw-Hill.

Barth, R. (1990). *Improving schools from within: Teachers, parents, and principals can make the difference.* San Francisco: Jossey-Bass.

Brown, J., & Moffett, C. (1999). *The hero's journey: How educators can transform schools and improve learning.* Alexandria, VA: Association for Supervision and Curriculum Development.

Brubaker, D. (1994). *Creative curriculum leadership.* Thousand Oaks, CA: Corwin.

Carroll, L. (1946). *Alice's adventures in wonderland.* New York: Random House.

Cooper, C., & Boyd, J. (2000). *Schools* as *collaborative learning communities.* Retrieved May 8, 2003, from www.vision.net.au/~globallearning/pages/Ifs/clc_artcle.html.

Deal, T., & Kennedy, A. (1982). *Corporate cultures: The rites and rituals of corporate life.* Reading, MA: Addison-Wesley.

Deal, T., & Peterson, K. (1994). *The leadership paradox: Balancing logic and artistry in schools.* San Francisco: Jossey-Bass.

DePree, M. (1997). *Leading without power.* San Francisco: Jossey-Bass.

Fullan, M. (1993). *Change forces: Probing the depths of educational reform.* Bristol, PA: Falmer.

Getzels, J., & Guba, E. (1957). Social behavior and the administrative process. *School Review, 65,* 423–441.

Heider, J. (1985). *The tao of leadership.* Atlanta, GA: Humanics Limited.

Hill, J., Pettit J., & Dawson, G. (1995). *Schools as learning communities.* A Discussion Paper. NSW Department of Education and Training. Retrieved May 8, 2003, from www.tdd.nsw.edu.au/resources/Papers/salcl.html.

Joyce, B., Wolf, J., & Calhoun, E. (1993). *The self-renewing school.* Alexandria, VA: Association for Supervision and Curriculum Development.

Kilmann, R., Saxton, M., & Serpa, R. (1985). Five key issues in understanding and changing culture. In Kilmann et al. (Eds.), *Gaining control of the corporate culture.* San Francisco: Jossey-Bass.

Kleine-Kracht, P. (1993). The principal in a learning community. *Journal of School Leadership, 3*(4), 391–399.

Kofman, F., & Senge, P. (1993). Communities of commitment: The heart of learning organizations. *Organizational Dynamics, 22*(2), 5–23.

Laswell, H. (1936). *Politics: Who gets what, when, and how.* New York: McGraw-Hill.

Likert, R. (1961). *New patterns of management.* New York: McGraw-Hill.

Maslow, A. (1965). *Eupsychian management.* Homewood, IL: Richard D. Irwin Inc. and Dorsey Press.

McGregor, D. (1960). *The human side of enterprise.* New York: McGraw-Hill.

Owens, R. (2001). *Organizational behavior in education.* Boston: Allyn and Bacon.

Schaefer, R. (1967). *The school as the center of inquiry.* New York: Harper Collins.

Schein, E. (1985). *Organizational culture and leadership.* San Francisco: Jossey-Bass.

Schlechty, P. (1997). *Inventing better schools: An action plan for educational reform.* San Francisco: Jossey-Bass.

Senge, P. (1990). *The fifth discipline: The art and practice of the learning organization.* New York: Currency Doubleday.

Senge, P., Kleiner, A., Roberts, C., Ross, R., & Smith, B. J. (1994). *The fifth discipline fieldbook: Strategies and tools for building a learning organization.* New York: Currency Doubleday.

Sergiovanni, T. (1996). *Leadership for the schoolhouse.* San Francisco: Jossey-Bass.

Uhl, S., & Perez-Selhs, M. (1995). The role of collaboration in school transformation: Two approaches. *Theory into Practice, 34*(4), 258–264.

van der Bogert, R. (1998). Learning in the schoolhouse. *New Directions in School Leadership, 7,* 71–83.

Wald, P., & Castleberry, M. (Eds.). (2000). *Educators as learners: Creating a professional learning community in your school.* Alexandria, VA: Association for Supervision and Curriculum Development.

5

The Leader as an Anthropologist

Ross Danis

Just as an anthropologist studies people, architecture, family communities, and cultural institutions, so should an effective school leader. While anthropologists have "digs" in a hill, school leaders' "digs" can be located at sporting events, the faculty lounge, the booster club meeting, and various other school-associated activities and social occasions. An administrator engaged in serious analysis of essential beliefs and core assumptions of a district's stakeholders will enable that leader to determine the driving factors of learning in the district. Rules and assumptions that enable a leader to study an organization's capacity to absorb and embed change and help an administrator "connect the dots" in a school system, similar to the manner in which an anthropologist identifies connections in a culture, are found in this chapter.

Demographers are the anthropologists of the 21st century. Who better understands us than the people who study our voting patterns, buying habits, and movie choices? The very fact that the advertisements in *Time* magazine vary by regions of the country is one significant example of the scope and specificity of the modern-day anthropologist as demographer.

Of course demographers produce data that is then used by others to sell ideas and products. Political analysts use demographic data to determine interests and formulate their positions. Marketing departments use demographic data to determine whether people are

reading *Smithsonian* or *People,* drinking Maxwell House or Star-
bucks, watching *Who Wants to Be a Millionaire* or *This Old House.*

In his book *The Clustered World,* demographer Michael J. Weiss
(2000) states that America is no longer a melting pot or a salad bowl
but, rather, a "fractured mirror" into which we all peer to see reflec-
tions of ourselves. Weiss has identified 61 "clusters" and has organized the United States by zip code and corresponding cluster. The
clusters have names like "Shot Guns and Pick Ups," "Kids and Cul
de Sacs," "Pools and Patios," and "Money and Brains."

From this clustering, Montclair, New Jersey, and Cambridge,
Massachusetts (they share a cluster: "Young Literati"), have more in
common than either one would have with communities only a few
miles away. In all likelihood, residents of Montclair and Cambridge
are watching similar television programs, eating the same nonfat yo-
gurt, shopping for organic foods, and driving similar cars.

To further grow this notion of demographer as anthropologist,
consider the computer technology that enables corporations to track
your cumulative buying habits. Purchase price range, time of day,
and color response can now be tracked so that over time, your taste
in books, movies, clothes, cars, coffee, politicians, and sexual habits
all become part of a very predictable package or cluster. Dot-coms
can use this data to market specifically to you in a way that is ex-
traordinarily tailored to your interests and values. Unbelievable, you
say? No, just good business.

LESSONS IN LEADERSHIP

How does this relate to education and, more specifically, educational
leadership? Educators often lament difficulties in implementing
change. Educators who are interested in facilitating a new organization of a school day or school year all point to the difficulty of implementing institutional change. Yet it can be easier if we first successfully market our proposals.

One must expect that selling a new way of thinking will be a daunting task. In a country where it is not uncommon to hear people say "we put children first," it could be argued that we put business first. The businesses that support products and stores are far more sophisticated and well financed than the people or the entire industry that runs America's schools. Consider the following: Every night after midnight, Wal-Mart stores analyze all of the previous day's receipts to make projections on which stores need to be shipped what merchandise, and which products should be ordered and which should be discontinued. In contrast, schools have a hard time making curricular revisions from annual test scores, often placing the blame for poor scores on students (the consumers in this metaphor).

Schools don't have the technology departments, the data-analysis knowledge and capacity, or the marketing departments to bridge a *selling of change* gap. Instead, resources flow into classrooms, books, supplies, and personnel. All the more reason why educational leaders should understand the culture of their community, the values of the organization, the board, the parents, the teachers, and the students. Thus, in order to communicate effectively and demonstrate sound judgment you must embrace a skill set that goes well beyond understanding curriculum and instruction, managerial skills, and the ability to delegate. Today's leader must also be a skilled anthropologist or, at the very least, a knowledgeable demographer.

KNOW THE NATIVES

How do educational leaders begin to access the cultural capital of an organization? When principals and superintendents are interviewed, they are asked about the experiences and assumptions that guide their approach to instructional models, children, personnel, community engagement, and board interaction. Once hired, how can a leader understand the history, folkways, mores, attitudes, and values of the organization and the community?

GET SOME ANSWERS

- Is there a *dissatisfied* contingent on the board that is looking to gain power? If so, are they looking for someone to carry their message forward?
- If the district has a motto or a slogan, what would it be? Is it "Any movement, any moment," or "We've always done it this way," or is it, "We get by on our reputation"?

UNDERSTAND THE LANGUAGE

What language is used to describe programs, people, parents, and students? When you ask teachers to describe students, if they talk about *the best and the brightest* then you know that they subscribe to a set of assumptions that embrace a *bell curve* notion of intelligence. If, in response to questions about children and their performance, you hear expressions such as, "What you see is what you get" then you know that the concept of "All students can learn" is not embraced. What if while conversing with a teacher regarding events, initiatives, programs, and reform efforts in the district, a teacher says, "This too shall pass," or "I've seen 'em come, and I've seen 'em go"? These phrases paint that picture for you.

About three years ago, I transitioned from a position as principal of a very progressive, artsy little elementary school into a position as the assistant superintendent of schools of an upper-middle-class, suburban, high-performing, sports-oriented, K–12 district. The progressive school could turn on a dime and was swarming with parents collaborating with teachers within its very synergistic and collaborative culture. In the new district, different things mattered. SAT scores mattered. The number of students getting accepted into Ivy League colleges mattered. The football team's record mattered. Test scores mattered. I quickly discovered that a practice in the new district was to group students by ability beginning in first grade. They formed those ability groups based upon standardized test scores, which began being collected in kindergarten. I questioned this practice almost immediately.

Of course the "we're not going to do this anymore" attitude is antithetical to an organization whose motto could have been "we've always done it this way." The district was a victim of its own reputation. Change was not something they believed they needed. Where I came from—the progressive, artsy little elementary school—change was the order of the day. In fact, if things stayed the same, there was a sense that something was remiss and that the school was falling behind. The previous community liked to be out in front. The parents and the teachers used to take pride in launching new programs and being a model for other schools in the area. This new district didn't like to make a move unless everyone else was *there* already. In fact, one of the mottos that could characterize the progressive, artsy elementary school's approach to change could have been "ready, fire, aim." The big, powerful, competitive K–12 district's approach to change could be characterized by not only the phrase "we've always done it this way" but also by "ready, aim, aim, aim, aim, aim. . . ."

Do you know your district's slogans and mottos? Is the district who they say they are, or is there something running below the surface that you need to discern before even proposing change? The district's language often reflects the myths, assumptions, and beliefs of the organization—listen closely. How is an educational leader going to sell (fill in your own initiative here) the concept of cooperative learning, multiple intelligence, critical thinking, brain-based instruction, and so on?

Just as an anthropologist studies people, artifacts, architecture, families, industries, and cultural institutions, leaders can and should do the same. Attend the football games and while you watch the game, listen to the conversations in the stands. Watch parents' reactions to the calls of the coach and notice the level of involvement the booster clubs have. As the new assistant superintendent, I stood next to the vice president of the board of education at a football game. He stood; I stood. He shouted "GO!" I shouted "GO!" Once, after our team moved the ball downfield in five-yard increments, no passes, all running, all brute force, he smiled and said to no one in particular, "Discipline; hard work. We may not be the best, but we keep our heads down and move forward an inch at a time." And he was right. (Note: Whenever a board member utters the phrase, "That's what this district is all about," pay attention.)

From that point forward, I started using words like *prudent* and phrases like *shoulder to shoulder* when describing how the district was promoting and preparing for a change in grouping patterns. Unfortunately, this was after an ineffective start that was memorialized in a newspaper headline that read "Assistant Superintendent says, 'District Outdated—Grouping to Be Dismantled.'" Where was Margaret Mead when I needed her?

EXAMINE COMMON PRACTICE

Parents. Do they volunteer? What is the nature and extent of their involvement? Are they engaged in meaningful curricular decisions or are they just doing the traditional fund-raising activities?

Grouping. Does the district group by ability? If so, in which grade? Grouping patterns are a quick litmus test of the district's attitude about the abilities of all children and their attitudes about the role of the school and the job of the teachers.

Testing. What does the testing program look like? How are tests used? Are they used to sort and categorize children, or are they used to make informed decisions about curriculum and delivery of instruction?

Technology. How is technology used? Is technology a tool, an end, or an expensive toy?

Art. What does the art program look like? Is it once a week? On a cart? Do students have opportunities to *experience* art or is it performance based? Are the art and music teachers included on instructional teams, if instructional teams exist?

The Teachers' Union. How many grievances have been filed against the district by the teachers union in the past few years? What was the nature of the grievances? Is there a story behind them that reflects a lack of trust in the administration or a cynicism on the part of the staff?

INFORMATION AND RELATIONSHIPS: FOUR RULES

Rule Number 1: Every conversation has significance. Several years ago, I was working to facilitate a multiage primary classroom as an alternative to the traditional single-graded primary grade program. In July, right before the September launch of the pilot program, one of the two project teachers told me that she was pregnant. I was happy for her but concerned that this news might trigger an exodus of parents who were not quite committed to having their children in the program. I needed time, so I asked, "Did you tell anyone else?" She said, "Just my teammate and my husband—oh, and my mother . . . and you." "Good," I said, "give me 48 hours to come up with a transition plan to announce to parents before this wonderful news becomes public." With that, I returned to my office. Five minutes later, the president of the PTA called and told me that she heard of the pregnancy and was removing her child from the program. So much for confidentiality.

Rule Number 2: A simple sentence becomes a chapter by the time it leaves the building, a book as it travels through the district, and an epic by the time it makes it around a few cul-de-sacs and soccer fields. When I first arrived at my office as the new assistant superintendent of schools, I toured the trailer that was temporarily (for the past 20 years) being used as the central office. Moving through the crowded space cluttered with file cabinets, copiers, and work tables, I made an offhand remark to a woman who later turned out to be my secretary. I said, "Wow, these computers are old!" By the time I officially started my job there, the only thing that everyone seemed to be talking about was that my first order of business was to replace all the old computers with new ones. How did that happen?

Rule Number 3: Spend more time in the stands watching so that when you do jump into the game, you carry the ball in the right direction. While I was still in the final days of being the principal of my warm, friendly, little elementary school, I was trying to attend evening meetings in the new district. I wanted to observe, get the lay of the land, and find out who the players were. As part of this learning experience, I attended a meeting of the technology committee. Shortly thereafter, I received an e-mail from the community member who was serving as chair of that committee. He asked if I knew anyone at a local telephone company who could be of assistance in securing a reduced Internet rate. I was so proud to know the vice president of a big Internet company. I e-mailed the chair that I did in fact know a very important and influential person and I would see if he could be of assistance.

When my e-mail program asked if I wanted to send this correspondence to *everyone*, I thought for a moment (clearly, not long enough) and hit the "yes" key. The next morning, as I walked out the front door, I turned to my wife and proudly said, "See, honey, I'm not even there yet and I am already making a difference." I arrived at my office to find an urgent message from the superintendent of the district I was supposedly helping. As it turned out, this technology committee was a rogue committee that had splintered off from the district-sanctioned technology committee. The district already had a reduced Internet rate, and I was told they didn't need that kind of help.

Rule Number 4: Look who's talking. Always know how information travels throughout a school, the district, and the community. Understanding communication networks helps you keep your finger on what people are thinking about, understand any dissidence, and understand the way in which you can use these networks to help disseminate your message clearly across different fronts.

When I was a new central office administrator, I started noticing that my recently retired predecessor was still taking the central office secretaries and the personnel director out to lunch. I also saw that one supervisor socialized with the former superintendent of schools. Some of these people were vocal opponents of the current superintendent who had hired me; thus, they were opponents of my programs and initiatives. I decided to intentionally get to know the supervisor; I even joined her and her husband and the former superintendent and his wife (a teacher in the district) for a social dinner. I noticed who was having coffee in whose office in the mornings when I walked through the high school. It didn't take long to start to connect the *communication dots*, and in fact, a phrase used in an argument against a program or initiative was sometimes parroted back to me later by two or three people in different buildings.

ASSUMPTION PYRAMIDS

As defined here, assumptions are *beliefs that you do not think about*. In fact, there is little examination of some of the assumptions that support the theories, concepts, laws, principles, strategies, and techniques that we educators so readily embrace and frequently adopt in schools.

This lack of examination of assumptions became crystal clear to me one day many years ago. I was working a booth at a teacher convention for an organization that developed and conducted workshops for teachers and administrators. We had presented to thousands of teachers from hundreds of schools over the course of several years. Many former conference attendees recognized us behind the booth at this convention and one even pointed at me and said, "Hey, you're that thumbs up–thumbs down guy." Searching my mind to make a connection, I realized that he was citing a technique that I had taught in a five-day workshop on a wide spectrum of concepts, strategies, and techniques. However, thumbs up–thumbs down was just one small piece of a greater strategy called "Checking for Understanding" that instructs us to monitor the learning and adjust the teaching. Thus, you would check for understanding and then use a technique called thumbs up–thumbs down.

And what about that concept of monitoring the learners and adjusting the teaching? That belongs to the UCLA model, also called *Instructional Theory into Practice* (Hunter, 1994) and sometimes just called the Hunter Model. Hunter's model is based on a theory, but a theory with no underpinnings in cognitive or humanistic psychology. Instead, the psychological theory that underlies the model is behavioral. It builds on a set of assumptions about children, teaching, and learning. The main assumption is that children should learn more, faster. More, faster is the underlying construct that supports the theory that supports the model that supports the concept that supports the strategy that supports the technique. If we had a different assumption, say learn less, slower—incidentally, one that many well-respected educators embrace—we might imagine a completely different infrastructure supporting a very different set of theories, models, concepts, strategies, and techniques.

What is important here is not the development of a deep understanding of the UCLA model or of the epistemological foundation of thumbs up–thumbs down technique. What is important is that you, as a school administrator (or aspiring school administrator), engage in a serious analytical examination of the essential beliefs and core assumptions that are driving the decisions regarding teaching and learning. These assumptions empower the direction of the administrative approach to instructional supervision, the available offerings of professional development opportunities, as well as the teachers' professional development plans and choices from within the range provided.

Entire systems of choices, networks of relationships, ways of being, pathways to knowledge, and frames of knowing all intersect at core beliefs and assumptions. Be aware. These assumptions influence our relationships in the faculty room, determine what we think is funny at the lunch table, and determine who we hire and who we fire. These assumptions cast the parameters of the relationships between the teachers union and the administration, as well as lurk underneath the selection of textbooks, and the organization of time within the school day.

Begin to identify the assumptions supporting practice, relationships, and approaches to teaching and learning in your school or district. Do you know the assumptions regarding teaching and learning in the school or district that you are leading or are about to lead? Perhaps you have never taken the time to think about such things. Perhaps you simply accept what *is* as the way it *is* everywhere, and you have decided either to adapt, or to try and change the organization to fit your vision of what a school should look like and how it should be organized to best deliver (or uncover) instruction.

IDENTIFYING ASSUMPTION PYRAMIDS

- *Show up and listen.* The life of a school leader is busy and full of scheduling demands that do not exist in many other professions, so I suspect that you may not like this next piece of advice, but it works. If you want to know the assumptions that guide practice in your school or in your district, then you have to be everywhere for a sustained period of time. Ask if you can attend a couple of finance committee meetings; see if you can participate in the superintendent's cabinet or roundtables; attend the late night negotiations (if permissible) with the bus driver association; go to the booster club meetings and parents' night; have coffee in the boiler room with the maintenance staff; start your day early in the construction trailer; sit in on a team-planning meeting with teachers; and above all else, spend time in the faculty room. Now, if all that mattered were showing up, everyone would be a knowledgeable demographer. The key is to show up and listen. Remember that you are on a learning expedition—a research project. You are not a casual observer or a friendly visitor. You are showing up with a purpose, and the purpose is to deeply and systematically learn the network of beliefs, assumptions, and values that support practice. Listen up.

- *Write it down.* You could use notecards to do this or simply keep a journal, but for a period of time you ought to take what might be called field notes. I prefer notecards as, after a mouth or so of sustained listening and recording observations, I can sit at the dining room table in the evening and organize the notecards into a variety of categories like a big puzzle. Over time, relationships begin to develop between people and ideas, between practice and belief, between teacher behavior and parent concerns, and between the booster clubs and the budget meetings. These patterns emerge only after getting close to the experiences, events, activities, and relationships within the school or district and then standing back far enough to discern these critical patterns.
- *Connect the dots.* Whenever a new idea is introduced, work backwards from the idea, through its conceptual, theoretical, and assumption base. Underneath all approaches to teaching and learning, to hiring, and to professional relationships is a set of values and beliefs. If your eye is on changing practice, you would be wise to work simultaneously on values and beliefs. The only way to begin this process on both a surface tactic and a subterranean strategy is to connect the dots between belief and practice.

FIX, FLOAT, FACILITATE, AND FUND

The last set of school leadership concepts to be explored in this chapter is what I simply call the 4 Fs. They are:

- Fix
- Float

- Facilitate
- Fund

From experience and observation, these four simple words have a high degree of verisimilitude, particularly as they relate to the experience of being a new administrator interested in change. Let's define each of them and then provide an example or two to help clarify the ideas in a way that makes visible their practical realities.

Fix. The most common mistake I see when observing the behavior of new administrators is that they often come into situations with ambitious plans to reform an instructional program. Do you know what people want when a new administrator enters an organization? They want some things to get fixed, and not necessarily abstract *things* either. More often than not, they are simple visible problems requiring concrete solutions.

A superintendent I know who really gets this concept discovered that school buses were regularly driving several miles out of their way to get fuel because the underground tank at the bus maintenance facility was no longer acceptable according to new environmental codes. He spent several days working with the town engineers, the department of environmental protection, the head of the transportation department, and the board of education. They devised an acceptable plan that would place an aboveground fuel storage tank on a concrete slab far enough away from the school buildings and the road. The responsible parties approved the plans within one month because the superintendent personally drove the individuals to the state capital and walked them to the right person, in the right department, of the appropriate agency to get the necessary approvals. By the end of month two the facility was built, and by the end of month three of his tenure the buses were filling their tanks at the maintenance yard. The first *fill up* was memorialized with a photo in the local newspaper, in which several hands—including the board president's, the transportation director's, and the town manager's—all held the nozzle of a pump about to be placed in a big yellow school bus.

This new superintendent fixed a significant and concrete problem, and for the next several months, people would take note of this in conversations. Parents, district maintenance workers, teachers, local business people, and under the lights in the parking lot at 11 p.m. after a board meeting, the board of education members who voted to hire him all talked about his active start.

When I first became an elementary school principal in 1993, I remember hearing that the 1969 addition to the school necessitated that the flagpole be torn down. It had never been replaced. Of course, I had big plans regarding curriculum mapping, professional development, and instituting a literature-based, primary grade program. But what did I do first? I organized a flagpole committee. We worked with the PTA and the town road department to raise the funds to install the new pole in front of the school. The local quilting club designed and stitched a school flag to fly under the American flag that was donated by the Boy Scouts. On Flag Day 1994, we had a ceremony to raise our two flags on our new flagpole in front of the school. The backhoe operator from the town attended with his wife and family. The Boy Scouts were there. So were the members of the quilting club, the PTA, several teachers, the mayor, representatives from the Veterans of Foreign Wars, and the local historian who had recently retired from the school after 40 years of service.

That same year, there was a lot of talk about the backup of buses and cars in the school parking lot in the morning, especially on rainy days when traffic volume naturally increased. Part of the problem was that parents would take a long time to say goodbye to their small children. We did not want to even venture into conversation about the need to drop off children quickly and move on. Instead, we brainstormed and determined that there should be an outside turn-around lane and a secondary dropoff at the bottom of the hill that leads up to the school, which would necessitate a supervisor at the bottom of the hill and traffic control in the parking area in front of the school.

The biggest challenge in our solution would be to keep a space open for cars to turn around and exit without having to wait behind the buses. So I manned the post in front of the orange cones, moving them each time to let a car through so another parent could exit down the hill. My post gave me many opportunities for quick hellos or to respond to questions about homework, field trips, and other everyday school concerns.

The level of detail in the stories of the fuel storage tank, the flagpole construction, and the turnaround lane is deliberate. I want to emphasize the critical importance of a commitment to the specifics and nuances of issues that might seem entirely unrelated to being an instructional leader. People, organizations, systems, communities, and an educational leader need to be able to fix problems and get things done together. The first grade teachers run out of construction paper before the end of the year? Fix it. The kindergarten classes have 267 students without any aides? Fix it. The music teacher has been on the list to have her room wired to the computer network, even though she has had the computer technology in her room sitting unused for two years? Even if you have to go in on Saturday and drag the wire yourself, make sure to fix it.

Float. Let's imagine that you've been fixing things for a while. You have cultivated some confidence and trust on the part of the staff, the board, and the community. Teachers have tested your commitment to them and the children. The school board is still pleased with their hiring choice and parents see you as fair and competent. Now is the time to float an idea: it could be that bold program to integrate subject matter, or the way to organize the curriculum so that it reflects a commitment to different ways of knowing, or the consideration of an alternative high school schedule that would have students taking subjects in 90-minute intervals rather than 40.

Float one or two ideas at a faculty meeting and then watch. Watch to see who responds favorably, takes notes, and asks perceptive questions. Watch especially to see who lingers after the meeting. If you notice two teachers who continue talking at a table for a few minutes after the meeting adjourns, these are the people that you need to meet with. They are your potential senators, soldiers, and receivers who could carry the ball forward in this game of progress and change.

If there is little demonstrated interest, then simply move on and recognize the fact that despite the value of an idea, its possibility for implementation is slim without the support and enthusiasm of the rank and file. Instead, double back and spend more time investing in relationships and expanding life experiences to help pull teachers into the flow of change. But if you do find a few takers, it is time to move to the next F in the 4 Fs.

Facilitate. It is time to invest in the professionals who have responded to a couple of ideas that have been floated in faculty meetings, study groups, or team-planning sessions. Whatever the topic, find a way for the professionals who demonstrate interest to become steeped in the literature surrounding the idea, issue, problem, or initiative. Send them to other schools to see what those ideas look like in practice. Send them to workshops and seminars. Give them release time if necessary and provide them with the resources they need to make well-reasoned recommendations to their colleagues or make a couple of board presentations on the topic while you look on from backstage. To facilitate professional engagement, commitment, and understanding is to embed the roots of the idea into the structural foundation of the organization. The idea gets carried forward by teams of professionals who experience the ideas through their own learning curve so that it is not grafted on to an external belief system; it is networked into their frame of knowing and their way of seeing. The new idea or initiative becomes part of the value and belief system that shapes and defines practice. With this approach must come the recognition that the end result might be quite different than the end result trial you imagined when you first floated the idea at the beginning of the process. Your job is to till the soil, fertilize the ground, plant the seeds, and then trust that what is taking place underneath the ground is going to result in growth that is healthy, needed, and wanted.

Fund. The problem with most new initiatives or change processes is that the support networks that were too intently applied throughout the formative stages often weaken from institutional fatigue precisely when the need for sustained support is most pronounced. A school district might commit to an approach to instruct, research and write curriculum, facilitate professional development, and purchase resources and support materials only to discover two years later that implementation is uneven, and in some cases completely sabotaged in creative and covert ways throughout the district. When program implementation fails to take root, teachers are often blamed, but the real culprits are the administrators. Critical to every initiative's success is sustained funding, and it is the administrator's job to make sure that support is sustained and institutionalized.

Where do ideas live and how do they get sustenance? They live in budget line items, so the best way to secure the institutional life of an idea that has turned into an initiative that has evolved into a program is to embed it in the budget. A school district's budget is the most reliable description of the values and beliefs of the system.

About 18 years ago, a group of teachers were interested in developing an outdoor education program that would foster self-confidence as well as a commitment to and a connection with nature. A secondary objective was to build relationships between groups of students converging from several different elementary schools into one large middle school. So began the Stokes trip. Stokes is the name of the state park that hosts this three-day retreat for hundreds of students and their teachers. During these three days, the students and their teachers participate in team-building activities and environmental experiences. They develop and present skits to each other after a communal dinner in the camp lodge. For several years, this program and experience had to be recreated from scratch, until it finally became part of the budget. To this day, there is a line item in the district's budget that simply says Stokes. Bus transportation, teacher honorariums, meals at the camp, and the consulting fees for the wilderness and environmental facilitators are all accounted for. Every year, the administration and the board of education approve the budget, simultaneously signaling de facto support for team building, fostering environmental connections, and confidence building for students as envisioned by a group of bold teacher leaders over 18 years ago.

I believe that the educational leader's best guarantee that a prized initiative will have a sustained life within a system is to secure ongoing funding. That commitment reflects in real terms a community's endorsement of a concept that may be carried over and discussed long after the originating design team, maverick principal, teacher leader, or project coordinator has retired or moved on.

There you have it: fix, float, facilitate, and fund. Four deceptively simple words that reflect a way of thinking about educational leadership and deliberately organizing, structuring, and framing organizations and systems to successfully adopt and sustain change.

SUMMARY

Much of what I present here has been learned the hard way—through strategic blunders or naively optimistic estimates of an organization's capacity to absorb and embrace change. Only through deliberate engagement in an active process of deep and sustained observation and analysis of the underlying beliefs and assumptions that support practice have I come to a more methodical—and more effective, I believe—means of traveling the path of an educational leader.

Part of the journey involves looking at systems through the lens of a demographer or anthropologist. Knowing the natives and understanding their language, their mores, and their folkways is the process of developing an ethnography that will richly inform your work as an educational leader. There are four rules related to understanding information and relationships within an organization. These include understanding that there is no such thing as a casual conversation and that a sentence is a book by the time it travels through an organization. It is important to watch and listen before acting and to keep track of how information moves through a system. Additionally, you now have a brief overview of what I have called Assumption Pyramids. The keys to understanding Assumption Pyramids includes listening, writing, and connecting the dots to establish patterns and networks within schools, districts, systems, and organizations.

Finally, I offer you a simple but sound template for forming your approach to the facilitation of change, particularly within the context of being a new administrator either in a district you know well or one that is completely unfamiliar. Fix, float, facilitate, and fund—the 4 Fs—can be a handy field guide. They will help you benefit from some of the lessons that I learned in a variety of settings and capacities throughout the years as a change-oriented educator actively engaged in educational reform and innovation.

REFERENCES

Hunter, M. (1994). *Instructional theory into practice*. Los Angeles, CA: University of California–Los Angeles.

Weiss, M. J. (2000). *The clustered world: How we live, what we buy, and what it all means about who we are*. New York, NY: Little, Brown.

6

Problem-Solving Leadership:
Demographics, Diversity, and Accountability

William L. Bainbridge

One of the greatest challenges facing school leadership today is the gap in student achievement. Demographics, diversity, and accountability are interrelated to the achievement gap that exists between White students and African American and Hispanic students. Historically, comparison of one school to another was used to measure student performance. This chapter focuses on the factors, historically seen, that negatively affect student performance and cause the achievement gap in a school. The factors viewed are focusing on race as an influence, in and of itself, as a major determinant of student achievement; the impact of parental education level; and the socioeconomic status of the family. The threat of comparison and its impact on student achievement is analyzed in this section as well.

All leaders are charged with the important task of solving the inevitable problems that arise in their organizations. Regardless of the organization, leaders must identify challenges, establish plans of action, and marshal the resources necessary to find workable solutions. Add to these factors expectations of boards, pressure from the public, demands of elected officials, the scrutiny of the media, and, of course, the necessity to ensure the successful education of children; and it becomes clear that school leaders face challenges that would bring the CEOs of many *Fortune* 500 companies to their knees.

In this chapter, we examine one of the greatest challenges facing school leaders today—the achievement gap between European

American (White) students and African American or Hispanic American students—in order to discuss three crucial interrelated topics: demographics, diversity, and accountability.

THE CHALLENGE OF CLOSING THE ACHIEVEMENT GAP

In this age of accountability, schools are frequently compared with other schools in order to provide a handy gauge for measuring performance. Many feel that such comparisons are essential in determining how students are doing compared with their peers at other schools. But often the demographic characteristics used to develop similar school or school system groups do not reflect the true picture of the students in any given school community. For example, two frequently used features, size and type (urban, rural, suburban) of the school system tell us very little about the kinds of students we actually find in the classrooms.

Performance is often compared among types of students as well. In order to assess how different groups of students compare to one another, most school systems track performance on achievement tests by race (African American, Hispanic American, Native American, Asian American, and White). Gender is also frequently used as a measuring stick. As school leaders are well aware, significant differences do appear between groups of students of different races and, to a lesser extent, between gender groups.

It is well established that African Americans, nationwide, generally perform below their White peers on standard achievement measures. The news media and academic press continue to report about the Black-White test score gap and lags in minority achievement. The mistaken impression almost always left is that gaps in performance are related to skin color. No single cause for these performance disparities has been determined, but no legitimate concrete evidence has ever been found that characteristics such as race affect students' cognitive ability. In fact, many studies of mixed-race children and children adopted by parents of differing races suggest that racial differences in test performance are mostly—perhaps entirely—environmental.

Some evidence suggests, in fact, that the very act of focusing on race influences students' ability to perform at their best. Compelling research from Stanford University shows that just knowing poor performance on a test could be used to confirm the lower ability of one group compared to another negatively affects performances. This phenomenon is referred to as the *stereotype threat*. When Black and White students were told they were being tested on their academic abilities, Blacks did worse than Whites. But when a control group was told the tests did not matter and were just a laboratory tool, the performance difference was eliminated.

The same findings apply to gender—and to other races. When women were told their performance was being compared to men's, women's scores went down. When White males were told their performance was being compared with that of Asian students, the White students' scores decreased. Take away the *threat* of comparison and all groups of students tend to perform at about the same levels, regardless of race or gender.

Disaggregating test scores by race may also have another unintended effect, that of increasing the inequality in educational content and quality between more affluent White schools and less affluent minority schools. Because teachers are often instructed to *bring up* scores for minority students, who also often happen to be poorer students, they set aside regular curriculum to spend days or even weeks of class time *teaching to the test*. Scores may go up for these students, but they have irrevocably lost crucial time needed for higher quality, higher level learning. This keeps the actual content knowledge of these groups of students below that of students who are not targeted for extra drills in test-taking skills. In other words, the attention paid to improving the test scores of minority students may actually reduce their overall performance and knowledge over time.

Far more relevant than race or gender in academic achievement are the education levels of students' parents (and other adults) and family socioeconomic status. Professionals have known for years that the greatest predictor of a child's success in school is the education level of the parents, particularly the mother. Research has shown that a relationship exists between school system effectiveness, the socioeconomic status of families in the community, and the education level of parents. Recent studies have suggested that early childhood experiences affect learning and development, with children from impoverished environments generally achieving at lower levels then those from more enriching situations.

A review of history illuminates the complex relationship between race, poverty, and education. Just a few generations ago, European Americans operated plantations via the abomination of slavery. Laws forbade educating slaves. When the slaves were emancipated in 1865, no GI Bill of Rights or Marshall Plan assisted their assimilation into the mainstream culture or workforce. For the most part, people of color lived in poverty without the means to become knowledgeable workers. When civil rights laws were passed in the 1960s, some affirmative action plans and laws were put in place, and a few philanthropic efforts were made to bridge the gap between the *haves* and the *have-nots*. Nevertheless, the gap between rich and poor has continued to grow, with the greatest adverse impacts on non-Whites. For example, African Americans are three times more likely than Whites to come from poor families.

The educational plight of the many non-English-speaking immigrants now entering the United States, of whatever ethnic group, is not much different. Their parents often have little formal education and lack the resources to provide academic stimulation and appropriate diet at home. Hispanic children, for example, are twice as likely to live in poverty than are White children. Those with educated parents tend to do much better on standardized tests. Living in poverty usually means that families are less able to afford good health care, nutritious food, or enriching cultural or educational experiences for their children.

The findings of noted University of Chicago neurologist Peter Huttenlocher (1997) emphasize the importance of mental stimulation in the home environment and the positive impact of a high-protein diet. The research of Huttenlocher and his colleagues over the past two decades has proved that most of the brain is *built* after birth. The fact is, young people who have well-educated parents, an academically stimulating home environment, and high-protein diets tend to do much better in school than youngsters without these benefits.

Although humans are born with very similar ranges of intelligence, the different nurturing processes that take place in the formative years have a tremendous impact on a child's ability to learn. Environmental factors continue to have a major impact on student achievement. Joseph Murphy (1999), professor of educational leadership at Ohio State University and president of the Ohio Principals' Leadership Academy, and his colleagues document a body of findings in the declining social welfare of children and their families:

> These data reveal a society populated increasingly by groups of citizens that historically have not fared well in this nation, especially ethnic minorities and citizens for whom English is a second language. Concomitantly, the percentage of youngsters affected by the ills of the world in which they live—for example, poverty, unemployment, illiteracy, crime, drug addiction, malnutrition, and poor physical health—is increasing. (p. 8)

Yet most studies that compare school districts unfairly use data such as total corporate and individual tax base per pupil or, as noted earlier, size and type of school, all of which are factors that have virtually no relationship to student learning outcomes. The fact is, students from high socioeconomic homes have great advantages in doing school work and are more likely to have access to computers and other learning devices in their many hours away from school.

Some surprising findings have indicated that the effects of
poverty extend beyond individual families. In schools with 25 percent of the student body living in poverty, all students, whether poor,
affluent, or in between, tend to do less well than students from
schools in affluent communities. Furthermore, even after a family
has achieved higher income levels, the effects of poverty can linger.
If two families have the same income levels, children from the family that became affluent more recently may lag behind children from
the family that has been affluent longer.

While there are many examples of highly successful people who
grew up in poverty and found mental stimulation and protein by
good fortune, research continues to indicate a direct correlation between the education level of the people in the home and amount of
protein in the diet and student success in school.

DEMOGRAPHICS

School characteristics such as building size, type (rural, urban, suburban), and tax base per pupil have been shown to have little or no relationship to the performance of individual students. Variables such
as parent education level, quality of diet, and access to stimulating
environments are related directly to the ability of individual students
to learn. Other factors used to compare students, such as race and
gender, have no real influence over cognitive ability or academic performance. Social and economic factors such as education levels and
families living in poverty have been shown to have greater influence
than any other characteristics on how well students do in school.

DIVERSITY

As our society has grown, the diversity in ethnic and cultural backgrounds and traditions in our schools has also grown. Our sensitiv-
ity to the needs of diverse groups of students is required in order for

us to be effective leaders and educators. Research has shown clearly, however, that focusing only on the characteristics that make students superficially different from one another is not only inaccurate but also may in fact hinder students' ability to achieve at their highest levels. Continuing to track performance based on race may actually contribute to the performance gap between African Americans and Whites. It is more accurate and beneficial to ensure that students who are the poorest and most educationally disadvantaged receive the greatest attention and resources. Understanding the interrelationship between poverty, family education levels, race, and achievement can help school leaders establish effective, equitable plans for distributing resources.

ACCOUNTABILITY

Since accountability often depends on comparison, it would seem wise to base comparisons on factors that really matter. Schools should be compared on an *apples-to-apples* basis, using community poverty and adult education levels as primary characteristics. With this kind of assessment, reasonable, attainable goals can be established, and more accurate gains in achievement can be measured and celebrated based on expected achievement levels for similar groups of students. Research shows that the gaps in achievement levels can be narrowed and learning can be improved for all groups of students—the true goal of any accountability program.

Nova Southeastern University Senior National Lecturer, M. Donald Thomas (1992) initiated the Audit of Educational Effectiveness while he was deputy state superintendent for accountability in South Carolina during the administration of then Governor Richard Riley. Thomas explained that schools should be compared with other schools that were mean-matched in terms of socioeconomic status. The audit has been conducted to improve student achievement through demographic, group-based, benchmarking accountability systems. In hundreds of school systems throughout the country, results of the audit have revealed a high correlation between student success on state-administered examinations and parent education level. Parent education level and poverty rates should be used as appropriate yardsticks in future research on this subject.

REFERENCES

Bainbridge, W. L. (2000, August). Is the test score gap really color-based? *The School Administrator,* p. 50.

Bruer, J. T. (1999). Neural connections—Some you use, some you lose. *Phi Delta Kappan, (81)*4, 264–277.

Bruer, J. T. (1998, February 27). A child is never too young to learn Mozart. *The Salt Lake Tribune.*

Huttenlocher, P. R., & Dabholkar, A. S. (1997). Regional differences in synaptogenesis in human cerebral cortex. *The Journal of Comparative Neurology, 38*(7), 167–178.

Jencks, C., & Phillips, M. (1998, September). The black-white test score gap: Why it persists and what can be done. *Education Week, 44,* 32.

Lewenton, P. C., Rose, S., & Kanin, L. J. (1984). *Not in our genes.* New York: Pantheon.

Lewin, D. J. (1995). Subtle clues elicit stereotypes' impact on black students. *Journal of NIH Research,* 24–26.

McNeil, L. M. (2000). Creating new inequalities: Contradictions of reform. *Phi Delta Kappan, (81),* 729–734.

Murphy, J., & Forsyth, P. S. (1999). *Educational administration: A decade of reform.* Thousand Oaks, CA: Corwin.

National Center for Education Statistics. (1999). *Early childhood longitudinal study, kindergarten class of 1998–1999.* Washington, DC: U.S. Department of Education.

Singham, M. (1998). The canary in the mine: The achievement gap between black and white students. *Phi Delta Kappan, (80),* 8–15.

Steele, C. M. (1992, April). Race and the schooling of black Americans. *Atlantic,* pp. 68–78.

Steele, C. M., & Aronson, J. (1995). Stereotype threat and the intellectual test performance of African Americans. *Journal of Personality and Social Psychology, 68,* 69–78.

Thomas, M. D. (1992, August). Acquiring essential data on schools. *The Effective Schools Report.*

Yiadero, D. (2000, March). Lags in minority achievement defy traditional explanations. *Education Week*, p. 1.

7

Leadership for Financial Adequacy

E. E. (Gene) Davis and M. Donald Thomas

In this chapter, the focus is on the leader's challenge to obtain adequate financial support in the current economic climate. The issue of equity in education finance programs has, historically, been the focus of the courts. Today, the issue question has changed from equity to adequacy. The role of the courts in this scenario is examined. The definition of adequacy by the courts creates the problem of deciding the level of funding needed: how is it computed? Five models for computing adequacy are identified, as well as the elements of a funding program. The connection between funding and educational quality and fairness is addressed.

The major challenge for educational leaders is the task of obtaining adequate financial support for public education. The task is made extremely difficult by economic interests that oppose the education of all children. As one legislator told one author, "Poverty is a self-selected condition and providing additional funds for undeserving children is wasteful." In addition, many policymakers see the education of low socioeconomic children as a threat to the economic advantage of their own children. To paraphrase *A Nation at Risk* (National Commission on Excellence in Education, 1983): If a foreign power wished to destroy democracy, there is no better way to do it than to provide inadequate support for public education. Education is the heart and soul of an enlightened and effective democracy.

Fiscally conservative segments of our population always look for cheap ways to improve education. Fads come and go, hand-in-hand with quick fixes that do not require adequate financial support. In addition, these same forces encourage legislation to promote vouchers, provide funds to religious-based private schools, and reduce public taxation. For decades, state supreme courts have dealt with the issue of *equity* in education finance programs. Recently, however, the question has become one of *adequacy*.

It all began with the West Virginia case, *Pauley* v. *Kelly* (1979). The court ruled that education is a fundamental right under state equal protection guarantees. It also said that some schools were "woefully inadequate." The court also stressed that responsibility for adequacy rested with the state and not with local communities. A long list of inadequacies were presented in the dicta of the justices.

Since 1979, a large number of states have experienced challenges to their school finance programs on the basis of adequacy. The question has been adjudicated in Alabama, Ohio, Texas, Missouri, New Jersey, Arkansas, Kentucky, Arizona, Wyoming, New Hampshire, South Carolina, and several other states. All have ruled that financial support for education was inadequate. The courts placed responsibility for establishing adequacy on the state legislative bodies.

Knowing that adequacy requires additional funds and higher taxes, legislators have not responded well. Therefore, the appellants have had to return to the court time and time again to obtain a proper remedy. In a majority of states, adequacy is yet to be established.

The courts have generally provided a uniform and clear definition of adequacy:

- An adequate program of educational services
- Adequate and safe school facilities
- Adequate increased funding for students with special needs
- Adequate educational support services, i.e., transportation

The problem is one of deciding the level of funding needed to achieve adequacy as defined by the various courts. School finance experts have established five methods for computing adequacy:

- The use of normative data
- The use of desired results
- The Resource Model
- The Education Priority Model
- The Econometric Model

All five methods have six features in common:

- Each student in the state receives an equal amount of dollars. This is the *base student cost* or the foundation program.
- The base student cost is increased by a multiplier for special needs students.
- Dollar allocations are increased for school districts that have a *higher cost of living*.
- Categorical funds are provided for *state interest* programs such as research.
- Sufficient state funds are provided for facilities and transportation services.
- All funds are distributed on a formula that utilizes weighted pupil units (WPUs) rather than student membership.

For state legislators, the most sensitive and difficult problem is that of determining how much money is needed to comply with court-defined adequacy. Thus, by utilizing any one of the five possible strategies, the money needed can be computed. How each model or method works is briefly discussed in subsequent paragraphs.

THE USE OF NORMATIVE DATA

This approach is probably the easiest to understand and the quickest in computing adequacy. The state first establishes what level of results it wishes to achieve. Then it finds school districts that achieve the desired results. The state then computes the average of expenditures made by the school districts that achieve the identified desired results. This average is then used to establish the *base student cost* or the foundation program.

The student base cost is then adjusted for special needs, for cost of living, and for other student demographic factors. The state distributes equal funds to all districts based on WPUs. WPUs are established by adding all students in membership adjusted by appropriate weightings or indexes.

THE USE OF DESIRED RESULTS

This approach is being used more and more now that accountability has become a major factor in education funding. The state decides what results the education system should deliver and then computes the money needed to achieve the desired results. The amount needed is computed by differentiating the cost required among various demographic student populations. The more disadvantaged a student population is, the more money is needed to achieve the state's determined results. Districts that fail to achieve the results are declared to be ineffective and are operated by the state.

The problem with this approach is that the state does not fund the system at an adequate level and attempts to achieve the desired results *on the cheap*. Not one state has ever funded at the level required to achieve state-determined results. All recommendations made by school finance experts using this model base have been rejected by state legislatures, most recently by the Ohio General Assembly. Currently, several legislative bodies are debating as to whether or not they can fund at a level required to achieve the desired results established by the state. The outlook is not optimistic.

THE RESOURCE MODEL

The Resource Model, often called the *input* model, establishes prototype schools and then computes the cost. The system requires that a number of decisions be made concerning the elements of each prototype school: elementary, middle, and high school. Decisions must be made related to class size, special personnel, technology, length of school year, and indexes for special needs students. Once the composition of each school is determined, salary levels must be established. A panel of educational experts examines all the *inputs* and salary levels and then computes the total cost needed to adequately operate each school.

Dividing the total cost by student membership provides the average cost per student. Dividing the total cost by the WPUs provides the *foundation cost* funds needed as a base to educate all regular students and special needs students. In addition, funds are provided for facilities and transportation.

THE EDUCATION PRIORITY MODEL

This model is a favorite of legislative bodies, particularly those in the more conservative states. The state establishes its priority for education based on the money it wishes to spend and places the burden on local communities to provide adequacy. The state decides the budget priority for education based simply on the money available. If adequacy is to be established, funds must be raised by increasing local taxes.

This approach is unfair to low-wealth districts. Generally, such districts cannot raise sufficient funds because of low-assessed valuations and lack of business property. The New Hampshire Supreme Court has ruled this system to be unconstitutional in that state.

The model also factors in indexes for economic conditions:

- Cost of living or labor market index
- Economy of scale as measured by school district size
- Property values and assessed valuations

ECONOMETRIC MODEL

The Econometric Model is generally the most expensive of the five methods. It establishes large indexes for a number of student characteristics, i.e., disadvantaged. Its application demands lengthy and expensive research as well as large amounts of new money. Conclusions obtained through the use of this model are controversial.

Economists who are pursuing the Econometric Model are attempting to construct a *cost function* for the state's educational system. The cost function is the money required to achieve a certain level of results with appropriate consideration given to different demographic characteristics of students and schools.

Using complicated mathematical formulas, the model establishes how much the state must spend to have school districts with state average demographics achieve at state average performance levels. The formulas can also be used to establish the required funds to have the average demographic school district achieve above the average state levels of performance. The higher the desired levels of performance, the greater is the money needed to achieve them.

The Econometric Model establishes adequacy as a more comprehensive set of educational services than that established by the other models. It gives consideration to many factors:

- Extra staff for extended and remedial services
- Teacher training activities
- School improvement efforts
- Parent education programs

- School readiness services
- Safety and school climate programs
- Indexes for sociological conditions:

  - Poverty
  - Disabilities
  - High risk
  - Limited English proficiency
  - Low income
  - Special needs

CONCLUSION

Recently, several states have attempted to establish a model adequacy school finance program. Resistance has come mainly from high-wealth school districts. In New Hampshire, it is especially strong from property rich cities like Portsmouth (Jiminez, 2000). The same reaction has occurred in Vermont. As reported in *Forbes* (McMenarnin, 1999) magazine: "This shift in funding has evidently not been accompanied by a gain in educational results. 'The good districts get worse, and the others don't get any better,' says Dartmouth College Professor William Fischel. 'They have made education worse on average.'" Much of the reaction is based on emotion and resistance is strong to an increase in taxes. It has little to do with educational quality and fairness.

A model school finance program, in any state where adequacy has not been established, will require an increase in taxes. The logic seems quite clear: if the financial support is not adequate, additional revenue is needed. Therefore, there is no need for legislators to have their lips watched for the message: *No more taxes*.

Here are the elements of an adequate financial program for public education in any state:

- A foundation program is necessary that would provide each nonweighted student $7,500. This figure is established by using normative data and studies conducted by other school financial experts like James Guthrie and John Augenblick (Visders, 1999). This is the *base student cost* and appears to be sufficient for an adequate program of educational services to a regular (nonweighted) student.

- The base student cost is increased each year by the cost of living index.
- The base student cost is increased by a system of weightings or indexes for the following:
    - Higher cost levels of education, i.e., high school
    - Higher cost programs, i.e., vocational
    - Students with disabilities
    - Students who are gifted
    - Students who live in poverty conditions
    - Students who have special needs, such as girls who are pregnant

Finally, the base student cost is adjusted in accordance with purchasing power of various regions. This is often called *cost of doing business*, *municipal overburden*, or *labor market index*. These four provisions constitute the elements of an adequate program of educational services. In addition, the state must also provide adequacy in facilities and transportation. To do so, the state should:

- Implement a statewide building program funded 100 percent by state funds. Building priorities would be established based on need by a state commission on school facilities.
- Establish a program of 100 percent funding for transportation. Routes established by local districts would have to comply with statewide criteria for both regular routes and activity routes.
- Provide adequacy in facilities and transportation and a program of educational services, with weightings for special conditions.

Some states may wish to go beyond the three components and establish categorical funding to promote the state's interests. These would include:

- State rules and regulations related to accountability structures
- Character education programs
- Staff development opportunities
- Research activities
- Retirement benefits

The most important question before the state legislators is: *How does the state fund education, especially an adequate education?* A model funding program consists of the following elements.

- *Adequacy of revenue.* The system is based on the entire wealth of the state and, as the court said, not on the *accident of geography.*
- *Ability to be understood.* The school finance program should be relatively easy to understand.
- *Protected from administrative manipulation.* School funds should be protected from manipulation by legislators or financial offices.
- *Based on current requirements.* The funding system should keep current with changing conditions and the introduction of new requirements.
- *Equity.* The finance program should provide an equitable distribution of funds to all districts based on needs—foundation program plus weightings.

To obtain sufficient revenue, the state should establish state-level taxes. Some states may wish to implement a plan that shares the cost between the state and local districts. The ratio of sharing, however, should not be less than 90 percent state responsibility. Local districts may wish to tax themselves at a higher level than the state-imposed tax. They should be permitted to do so and should be allowed to keep the entire collected revenue.

Adequacy for public education has never been established, nor have we ever *thrown money at schools*. It would be a great moral act if we did it just once. In the absence of doing that, however, it is in our nation's interest to establish an educational system that can adequately educate our children and our young people. It does, however, require courage and duty from state legislative bodies. In addition, it requires forceful and aggressive leadership by educators!

REFERENCES

Jiminez, R. (2000, January 2). Granite state tax plan pleases few. *The Boston Sunday Globe.*

McMenamin, B. (1999, December 13). Robin Hood doesn't approve. *Forbes*, pp. 102–105.

National Commission on Excellence in Education. (1983). *A nation at risk.* Washington, DC: Author.

Pauley v. Kelley, 162 W. Va. 672, 255 S.E.2d 859 (1979).

Visders, D. (1999, September 29). How much is enough? *Education Week.*

8

Exemplary Leadership: A Process

Karen M. Dyer

The definition of a successful leader varies among individuals, but all have a common goal: To be the best leader one can be. "Desire + skill + experience" must be joined by a belief and an attitude that exemplary leadership is a process, not an event. In this chapter, a successful leader is defined as one who uses diplomacy and tact with those they lead in order to identify common ground and share a created purpose. Also identified in this chapter are nine paradoxes that leaders encounter in the process of developing exemplary leadership. The exemplary leader enjoys the meaningful work that he or she accomplishes which improves the life of a child, and in the end, that is all that really matters.

It would be rare to find someone who goes into educational administration striving to be anything less than a competent, effective leader. While indicators of success vary among individuals (e.g., improved student achievement, contract renewals, salary increases, recognition, favorable evaluations), the goal is ultimately the same—to be the best leader that one can be. Most school administrators come into their positions with a fair amount of skill often augmented with experiences that have bearing either directly (assistant superintendent, assistant principal, teacher leader) or indirectly (business executive, nonprofit director, military expertise) on their ability to satisfy the demands of the role. It would appear then that a formula of desire + skill + experience would equal success.

However, this is not always the case. Each of these components is necessary, but none is sufficient either independently or interdependently. They must be joined by a belief and an attitude that exemplary leadership, much like change, is a process, not an event. They are necessary ingredients to the same recipe but each set of directions will be different.

GO PLACIDLY AMID THE NOISE AND HASTE AND REMEMBER WHAT PEACE THERE MAY BE IN SILENCE

So begins *Desiderata*, Max Ehrmann's (1927) poem that was popular in the late 1960s and early 1970s. Interpretations of the poem and its meaning abound. While many purport that this piece of writing is an inspirational commentary on love, it can also be argued that it serves as a lesson for educational leaders on how to strive toward becoming exemplars of success in leading change in their districts and organizations.

The successful educational leader understands that in any system experiencing change there is generally chaos before there is order. Change theorist William Bridges (1991) refers to this as *the wilderness*. The successful leader, on his or her road to becoming exemplary, recognizes that it is critical to have the ability to control stress, to exhibit a calming influence during crises, and to hide frustrating behaviors such as defensiveness, irritation, overreaction, and anger when confronted by disorder or confusion. A teacher recounts:

> Twenty-five years ago I experienced a teacher's worst nightmare. A student of mine died while on a school outing. I recall the mass of emotions swirling around in my head and in the pit of my stomach. I was both scared and angry, grieving and guilty, even knowing in my more rational moments that there wasn't anything that I had done or failed to do that had contributed to this tragedy. Yet, I was anxious to find someone or something to blame, even if it meant myself. Be-

tween talking to the police and the coroner, worrying about the other students, anticipating and dreading the conversation with the deceased child's parents, I still remember telephoning my principal not knowing what to expect, but anxious nonetheless.

What I found was comfort and strength in the tone of his voice and in his choice of words. The first person he asked about was me. He kept assuring me that everything would be all right. Next, he inquired about the rest of the students, and then we began working on next steps. All around me there seemed to be noise and clamor. Yet, in that phone booth I found assurance and support. I've never met anyone else in or out of education who could make so much sense out of so much bedlam. He was more than my principal; he was my hero.

AS FAR AS POSSIBLE WITHOUT SURRENDER
BE ON GOOD TERMS WITH ALL PERSONS

Leadership is everybody's business. It is not just the formal leader who has a vision for a particular change initiative. Those implementing the change must also have a vision of how relevant and meaningful this change is to their own work realities.

A school or district administrator, by the very nature of his or her title, possesses the power of position. However, this particular authority generally engenders results through compliance. Unfortunately, compliant behavior, unlike committed behavior, must be supervised—maintained through monitoring or through the element of fear. Extraordinary leaders understand that for a change effort to be internalized by people in the organization and subsequently institutionalized, a combination of personal power alone with positional power must be used to help people gain commitment. The leader acknowledges through his or her behavior how critical it is for people to support the change effort not because it is the will of the leader, or because of a need to please the leader, or because of fear of the leader, but because it is what is best for the school, district, and all of the stakeholders—especially students.

Great leaders understand that lasting results cannot be achieved by creating unnecessarily adversarial relationships. The exemplary leader has learned through observation, coaching, mentoring, and/or trial and error the importance of using diplomacy and tact in working with disparate groups. In addition to skill in relating to diverse groups of people, the effective leader is able to help those constituents who hold different values, beliefs, and opinions; to identify common ground; to confront generalized assumptions; and to create shared purpose.

Clark is regarded as a highly successful superintendent. He is consistently being sought after by well-known *head hunting* groups. He is known for the constructive and effective relationships that he has with board members, direct reports, and peers and with others both within and outside of his organization. While he has been revered for his interpersonal skills, he is respected for his leadership. People comment that he is tough and willing to confront issues head-on. However, he is talented in getting others to believe in where he is encouraging them to go. A member of his staff remarked, "He's got his head in the clouds but his feet on the ground." Said one union leader,

> I've dealt with several superintendents and what makes him stand out far above the others is how you feel after a day of negotiations. He may not have agreed with you, and he may not have even yielded, but all the while you felt respected.

SPEAK YOUR TRUTH QUIETLY AND CLEARLY; AND LISTEN TO OTHERS, EVEN THE DULL AND IGNORANT; THEY, TOO, HAVE THEIR STORY

Most people are aware of the basics of good listening: don't interrupt; paraphrase; follow-up with probing questions; make eye contact; show respect for differing opinions; be aware of body language such as facial expressions, fidgeting, position of arms, proximity. A common fault of even effective leaders is that of only listening when one is interested or when one has a need to know what is being said or has a connection to the person doing the talking,, or worse, simply listening for the other party to take a breath so as to interject one's own opinion. It is hard to listen to people you do not like or to those who are disorganized in their thinking, are long-winded, are chronic complainers, or are problem unloaders. In addition, it is difficult to listen when one is being criticized or personally attacked.

Exemplary leadership requires practicing attentive and active listening, not selective listening for key points, even with those who tend to waste a lot of time. According to Lombardo and Eichinger (1998), the leader sometimes needs to take on the role of a teacher, helping the person who is doing the talking to craft their communication in a more acceptable way. It is acceptable to interrupt, to summarize, or to let them know that next time they might want to be shorter and/or come with less data. The effective leader does not signal that he or she is not listening or is not interested. He or she will ask questions to help the speaker focus; he or she will encourage people to write down their problems and solutions and will paraphrase without necessarily offering advice.

When it is the leader who is being criticized or personally attacked, the most competent administrator lets the other side vent without reaction—allowing the other party to keep talking—even if what is being said is untrue. By nodding, (I hear you, not I agree with you), by asking clarifying questions, and by controlling defensiveness, one is able to satisfy the task of accurately understanding what the other person is trying to communicate.

A parent recalls his dealing with an associate superintendent:

The board of education having just undergone redistricting, announced that 250 of our students would need to attend another high school. We took our case to the school board, to the media, and even pursued a legal challenge, but we seemed to get little or no relief. A group of about 25 of us, as a last act of frustration, decided to picket the central office administration building. The superintendent refused to meet with us, and that just seemed to make it worse. He sent his associate to meet with us. I still can remember Dr. Beard escorting us into a conference room where we all sat around a large table. He set up ground rules that only one person could speak at a time, that he would suspend the meeting if at anytime profanity was used, and he would not tolerate any personal attacks. He promised to stay as long as we had something to say.

For three and a half hours he listened, took notes, and periodically asked us questions. Afterwards he told us that if we would wait for about an hour, he would get some answers to as many of our questions and concerns as he could. He returned in exactly one hour. Some of the answers were still not what we wanted to hear, but we all felt that finally someone had cared enough about our concerns to listen. Our students still ended up being transferred, but each one of us still remembers and appreciates what Dr. Beard did for us that day. He listened.

IF YOU COMPARE YOURSELF WITH OTHERS, YOU WILL BECOME VAIN AND BITTER; FOR ALWAYS THERE WILL BE GREATER AND LESSER PERSONS THAN YOURSELF

Most leaders know that during the planning, initiation, or implementation stages of a change initiative it is important to both lead and manage staff; the exemplary leader knows that one must also lead and manage their own superior(s) whether boss, supervisor, or governing board. Knowing one's boss, understanding his or her strengths and weaknesses, being able to identify the boss' trigger points, and learning to adapt to his or her style of leadership is crucial in situations involving change even if the particular change effort has been mandated by the boss.

The exceptional leader always positions himself or herself to learn from the boss, sometimes what to do, sometimes what not to do. The leader is open to both positive and negative feedback and seeks more to understand than just to be understood. The leader of excellence is loyal and supportive and acknowledges that disagreements with one's superiors are not to be publicized.

Wise leaders recognize that information is motivating and empowering in that it assists in decision making and connects people to the work. The lack of information is disempowering and can lead to organizational dysfunction. Not sharing appropriate data, especially with one's boss, is a dangerous precedent that can lead to poor relationships and possible abortive behaviors such as sabotage and/or termination.

From a former assistant principal:

My principal told me the first day on the job that with the exception of agreed upon confidences, 'If I know it, you will know it. And, I expect the same from you.' This was our practice for the three years that we worked together. I learned from her, and I think that she learned from me—at least she told me that she had. In the beginning, staff, parents, and even students would try to 'divide and conquer.' They learned quickly that even though we had different personalities and leadership styles and that we occasionally disagreed on something, the other always knew what was going on—including what the other person's thoughts on a subject might be. I continued this practice with my own assistant principals once I became the formal leader of my own school. I suppose that I wouldn't know how to behave any differently.

One source of strength is self-knowledge. Seeking feedback and being open to criticism signals to others that you not only value their opinions of you, but, most important, that you value yourself in becoming the most effective leader possible. Exemplary leadership demands that one not wait for annual performance reviews or sentiment surveys. Rather, the leader looks to get feedback from other venues as well, such as 360-degree surveys, mentors, peer reviews, and informal conversations, to name a few.

Karen M. Dyer

ENJOY YOUR ACHIEVEMENTS AS WELL AS YOUR PLANS

According to Richard Farson (1996), "Paradoxes are seeming absurdities. And our natural inclination when confronted with paradoxes is to attempt to resolve them, to create the familiar out of the strange, to rationalize them" (p. 13). Planning, for many school administrators, is one of these paradoxes. Everyone is expected to plan as a precursor to change. However, if one is too rooted in the plans and is not receptive to flexibility, a change effort may fail. Planning is not the only paradox that leaders encounter. Deal and Patterson (1994) identify nine paradoxes that leaders encounter in the process of developing exemplary leadership.

The paradox of pride. The exemplary leader is proud of his or her accomplishments and of the journey to achieving those accomplishment, *and* the exemplary leader is humbled by the knowledge that there is always room for improvement.

The paradox of role expectations. The effective leader accepts that sometimes you do what you are told, *and* sometimes effective leaders have to practice a little *creative insubordination*.

The paradox of performance. The extraordinary leader understands that everyone is fallible and that occasional mistakes are expected, *and* the extraordinary leader isn't fooled in thinking that he or she isn't always expected to do it right.

The paradox of problem perception. The great leader realizes that no matter how skilled he or she is in anticipating them, problems are unavoidable, *and* the great leader knows that problems must be avoided whenever and wherever possible.

The paradox of control. The savvy leader is in control at all times, *and* the savvy leader knows that he or she must often concede control so that others can lead.

The paradox of concern. The distinguished leader is tender and cares for individuals in the organization, *and* the distinguished leader is tough and cares about the organization.

The paradox of decision making. The exceptional leader does not make decisions until he or she has figured it all out, *and* the exceptional leader sometimes acts before he or she is sure.

The paradox of delegation. The superior leader delegates to others, *and* the superior leader does it all himself or herself, if necessary.

The paradox of resource allocation. The ideal leader knows the importance of distributing resources equally, *and* the ideal leader knows the importance of distributing resources where they are needed most.

The leader who is skilled at the art of reconciling paradoxes understands that depending upon the situation, one must be able to act in ways that are seemingly contradictory without confusing people or appearing "wishy-washy."

Because effectiveness as an educational leader should be an ongoing pursuit, one needs to be cautious that intermittent or even consistent success does not become fodder for arrogance. The honest leader subscribes to the adage, *You meet the same people going up as you do going down.* John Heider (1995) describes it this way:

> If you measure success in terms of praise and criticism, your anxiety will be endless. If the group applauds one thing you do, and then you feel good, you will worry if they do not applaud as loudly the next time. If they are critical, if they argue or complain, you will feel hurt. Either way, you are anxious and dependent. (p. 25)

NURTURE STRENGTH OF SPIRIT TO SHIELD YOU IN SUDDEN MISFORTUNE. . . . MANY FEARS ARE BORN OF FATIGUE AND LONELINESS

Leadership is not easy, especially during times of change, periods of conflict, when trust has been violated, or when the issues are those of integrity. Exemplary leadership cannot be sustained unless there are periods set aside for reflection, renewal, and relaxation.

Leaders are often reminded about balance. Having balance in one's life, however, does not imply that everything needs to be equally divided. The concept of balance is unique to each individual and means finding what is reasonable in terms of time, energy, and interest. There are multiple dimensions to balance: family, career/work, self, relationships, recreation, emotional health, spiritual well-being, health/exercise, intellectual stimulation, hobbies, pets, etc.

Exemplary leadership, especially during times of change and transition, means that sometimes you have to say *no* to people and activities that are enjoyable, valued, and perhaps even worthwhile. Saying *no* is not about being mean or insensitive or depriving oneself or others. Saying *no* is about setting priorities. Unfortunately, others may take it personally even when the intent is simply to nurture one's own spirit. The leader can ease the disappointment of ungratified expectations by shaping perspectives and relating that these priorities, though significant, may well be situational and could change at a later time. A superintendent commented,

> A few years ago, prior to becoming a superintendent, I went through a period where I began to experience some stress-related symptoms that had me worried. Special attention to diet, exercise, sleep, and meditation did not seem to minimize the symptoms. My anxieties, exacerbated by my physical symptoms, began to affect my self-esteem and confidence in my own competence. After talking with my primary care physician, I sought out the services of a counselor. He told me that for two weeks he wanted me to say *no* to any person or task that could not be finished in 20 minutes or less. He gave me permission, of course, to deal with work and family obligations that went beyond this time frame, but for all others I was limited to 20 minutes.
>
> This simple strategy worked so well that by the end of the two weeks, my symptoms had disappeared. It was so freeing to have permission to say *no*. I've matured a lot since then and find that I no longer require someone else's permission to say *no*. However, whenever I start experiencing some of those same symptoms, I reflect on

all that I am doing and occasionally I put myself on a two-hour, two-day, two-week, or two-month regimen of *just say no.*

STRIVE TO BE HAPPY

Exemplary leadership acknowledges that when all is said and done, it will not matter how much money you made, the number of contracts that you had renewed, the successful programs that you ran, or the various honors that you received. What will matter is that you did meaningful work that you enjoyed. What will matter is that the changes you envisioned, initiated, implemented, and sustained made a difference in the life of a child. And in retirement, it will matter that you know that our nation was well served by what you did.

REFERENCES

Bridges, W. (1991). *Managing transitions.* Reading, NM: Addison-Wesley.

Deal, T., & Peterson, K. (1994). *The leadership paradox: Balancing logic and artistry in schools.* San Francisco: Jossey-Bass.

Ehrmann, M. (1927). *Desiderata.* Toronto, CN: Crown.

Farson, R. (1996). *Management of the absurd.* New York: Touchstone.

Heider, J. (1995). *The tao of leadership: Leadership strategies for a new age.* New York: Bantam.

Lombardo, M. M., & Eichinger, R. W. (1998). *For your improvement: A development and coaching guide.* Minneapolis: Lominger.

9

Leadership and the Law

T. C. "Chris" Mattocks

Leadership, in all its forms, must operate under a giant umbrella of laws, rules, and regulations that can be referred to as public policy. Whether that policy is mandated in the U.S. Constitution, formulated by Congress, enacted by state legislatures, or adopted by local school boards or school committees, it basically becomes the law of the land under which leadership must be shaped. While no one argues that education leaders should be left to follow their own moral compass in the school setting, these policies have been both a bane and a blessing to the profession. Highlighted in this chapter are some of the more obvious impacts that public policy on the federal, state, and local level has had on who lead today's school systems.

FEDERAL POLICY

From the earliest days of settlement in America, there was a feeling that the education of young people was going to be essential to the well-being of society; although there were differences in opinion as to who should bear the burden of providing that education. In general, the colonists of the north believed that education of all children should be seen as beneficial to society and that taxes should be levied to support this educational effort. However, the southern colonists believed that only children of well-to-do parents deserved to be educated, and these parents sent their children to church-related or private schools to preserve their exalted status. In both instances, the "American colonies had to overcome the accepted pattern of the class-oriented English educational system in which free and universal education was beyond the eye of most progressive governmental leaders" (Alexander & Alexander, 2001, p. 22).

As tensions in the colonies grew and eventually led to the Revolutionary War, the thinking of local leaders came under the influence of the Age of Enlightenment. John Adams, James Madison, and Thomas Jefferson adhered to Jean Jacques Rousseau's belief that education and citizenship were inexorably intertwined (Rousseau, 1973). In the middle decades of the 1700s, this feeling developed into the idea that a free system of education would provide for a general increase in knowledge for the youth, would engender new learning for others in society, and would certainly cultivate the democratic ideals of government.

Obviously, these framers of the Constitution were not against education but felt that such an important matter should be a function of the states to fund and control so that the federal government could not be accused of forging a national *agenda* in this area. Given that the signers present at our nation's beginning were more interested in federal policies dealing with commerce, banking, and military matters, this is understandable. Thomas Jefferson's words in his Bill for the More General Diffusion of Knowledge (1779) would later find their way into the Virginia Bill of Rights and would accurately define the mood at the signing of the Declaration of Independence.

> That free government rests, and does all progress, upon the broadest possible diffusion of knowledge, and that the Commonwealth should avail itself of those talents which nature has sown so liberally among its people by assuring the opportunity for their fullest development by an effective system of education throughout the Commonwealth. (The Constitution of Virginia, 1971)

The conundrum is the extent to which the federal government has now entered into the educational arena at all levels, considering the conscious omission of such an important matter by the founding fathers.

Even though the Constitution is silent regarding education, it does affect leadership in the school. The primary effect comes from the first 10 articles found in the Bill of Rights, which were originally adopted as amendments to the Constitution by the Constitutional Convention and sent to the states for ratification starting in 1790. James Madison had successfully argued during the Constitutional Convention in Philadelphia in 1787 that the Constitution should only deal with governmental matters. Other signers, notably Jefferson, argued that the document should also contain statements regarding the rights of individual citizens. It was more than a decade before Jefferson finally convinced Madison of the importance of what have come to be known as one's civil rights.

Several articles in the Bill of Rights impact the school on a daily basis, in particular the First, Fourth, and Fourteenth Amendments, or the "Big Three." While each of the amendments seems fairly simple in construction, their application in the school setting has been anything but simple. Time and time again the courts have been asked to interpret the intent of the founding fathers—more than 200 years ago—to the actions of school-age children in the 20th and 21st centuries. The resulting decisions have, in many cases, caused a rift in allowable student behavior for different sections of our nation. School leaders are often left wondering which court decision applies to their particular situation on any given day.

THE FIRST AMENDMENT

It was mere coincidence that the First Amendment was the first to play a role in the life of a school leader. John Adams was one of the majority of representatives at the Constitutional Convention who realized that the diversity of religious backgrounds of the delegates was so great that any mention of religion in the Constitution would

surely doom passage of the document by the states. He assumed that
if the issue of religion were not mentioned in the Constitution, the
state and religion would both be better off. He stated his belief that
"Congress will never meddle with religion further than to say their
own prayers, and to fast and to give thanks once a year (cited in
Green, 1941, p. 83).

Issues dealing with student speech, student religious expression,
and student assembly are now all part of a school leader's life. The
most difficult concept for school personnel to master, as agents of
the government, is that the government cannot be a player in any
part of nondisruptive student religious expression. In apposition to
this is the fact that the government must be a player in student free
speech issues, even if such issues are disruptive to the status quo.
Both issues deal with student speech, but the school leader must be
able to distinguish when to get involved and when to stay on the
sidelines.

Beginning in the early 1940s, U.S. Supreme Court decisions on
student participation in the Pledge of Allegiance began shaping student religious expression in the schoolhouse (U.S. 624, 1943). The
Court decided in the early 1960s that any state-constructed prayer or
Bible readings in the school setting were in violation of the First
Amendment (U.S. 421, 1962; U.S. 203, 1963). In 1992, the Court
decided that a nonsectarian cleric-led prayer at a middle school graduation ceremony was a violation of the First Amendment (U.S. 507,
1992), although some authors believe there is an acceptable middle
ground for student-initiated, student-led prayer at a graduation ceremony (Mattocks, 2001).

Student free speech issues during the Vietnam War gave rise to
one of the most famous quotes when the Supreme Court noted that
"students do not lose their constitutional rights at the schoolhouse
door" (U.S. 503, 1969). In this classic case of how much tolerance
school leaders must have for student speech that does not disrupt the
school setting, students who were in favor of the late Sen. Robert
Kennedy's efforts for a peaceable resolution to the Vietnam War

wore black armbands as a sign of their support for that position. The students did not disrupt any school activities, nor did they vocalize their positions in any class. They were suspended for their behavior by school administrators who felt that their actions could have been detrimental to the daily school operation.

The Court, in rendering its decision that the students were unfairly excluded from school, noted that no disruption had occurred during the students' activities, nor could the school administrators point to any reliable information that disruption was imminent at the time. While it may be said that the rise of student rights in the public school setting began with the *Barnette* (1943) decision, they were certainly solidified with the *Tinker* (1969) decision.

THE FOURTH AMENDMENT

The second of the "Big Three," the Fourth Amendment, is perhaps the most sensitive of the group in that it deals with searches of a student's locker, car, backpack, clothing, or body. The Fourth Amendment was originally drafted to protect citizens against unreasonable searches unless there is *probable cause* for such a search. When the amendment was drafted and ratified in the late 18th century, citizens of the new nation still had vivid memories of British soldiers breaking into their homes without provocation or reason and taking whatever they desired. The courts have come to realize that the right to privacy is not absolute; it is relative. The government must have the right to enforce its laws, just as schools must have the right to enforce their rules. The balancing factors are the purpose of the search, who is doing the searching, and what is being searched.

The U.S. Supreme Court held in 1985 that "schools were special environments where school officials have the duty and responsibility for the safety, health, and learning of children" (U.S. 325, 1985). Searches that might be illegal in other settings for similar circumstances would be sanctioned in schools by the courts. Because of the increased "duty and responsibility" noted in the *TLO* (1985) decision, less demanding standards are applied by the courts to searches conducted by school officials. Even prior to the *TLO* decision, courts had held that students had no reasonable expectation of privacy in lockers, desks, or other school property provided for storage of their belongings.

Where police and other such authorities have the burden of showing *probable cause*, schools have a lesser standard of *reasonable suspicion*. School officials must basically answer two questions to determine the legality of any search: (1) Was the search *justified* at its inception; that is, was there reasonable suspicion that something was going on? (2) Was the search *reasonable* in scope; was the search more intrusive than it had to be? The danger for school officials who go beyond the well-defined boundaries of reasonable suspicion is that the court will not only prevent the use of evidence found in an illegal search but it could also conclude that school officials be held *personally liable* for any illegal search. Such a finding could allow students to sue school officials for damages.

THE FOURTEENTH AMENDMENT

The Fourteenth Amendment is a relative latecomer to the body of amendments to the Constitution. It was ratified by the states in 1868 to ensure the constitutionality of Reconstruction statutes that had been enacted to proscribe racial discrimination after the Civil War. Of the three sections of the amendment, the last two are most telling for school districts:

- No state shall deprive any person of life, liberty, or property without due process of law.
- No state shall deny to any person within its jurisdiction the equal protection of the laws.

The Fourteenth Amendment is the legal *door* through which school officials must proceed in cases involving everything from the denial of a student's right to attend school to an employee's right to continued employment with the school district. In general, it demands that school officials not be arbitrary, unreasonable, or discriminatory in their actions dealing with the discipline or sanction of others. It is important to note that protection is given to *persons,* not just citizens.

Both students and teachers have *property rights* when it comes to school. A student's property right to an education is created by state legislatures when they require compulsory student attendance, generally from ages 7 to 16. If the student is required by law to be in school, then it takes some fairly extreme behavior for the school to deny him or her that right. The school official must also be cognizant that violations of school rules usually do not merit the attention of local law enforcement, but a student's violation of state criminal statutes may also be a violation of school rules. In most instances, this is not seen as *double jeopardy* for the student since violation of both criminal statutes and school policy may result in two different forms of sanction.

Student due process rights are not absolute and depend on the violation under consideration. The seminal case involving student due process rights, *Goss v. Lopez* (1975), answered the question about whether a student could be suspended from school for up to 10 days without a hearing prior to the suspension or within 72 hours thereafter. Another question was whether an Ohio law that permitted school principals to suspend a student for up to 10 days without a hearing amounted to a lack of due process. The Court agreed that students must at least be notified and given a hearing "as soon after the suspension as practicable." The Court, however, also established, by default, the well-known standard that a school may suspend a student for up to 10 days simply by confronting a student with his or her misbehavior, allowing the student to tell his or her side of the story and then imposing the suspension. The

Court opined that "longer suspensions or expulsions for the remainder of the school term, or permanently, may require more formal procedures."

Teacher property interest rights in employment have their foundation in the original intent of the Bill of Rights. James Madison was very explicit in his idea that not only does a man have "a right to his property" but he also has "a property in his rights" (Levy, 1988, p. 266). Madison believed that a man had a property in his opinions and the right to freely communicate them when he stated,

> He has a property of peculiar value in his religious opinions, and in the profession and practices dictated by them. He has the property very dear to him in the safety and liberty of his person. He has an equal property in the free use of his faculties and free choice of the objects on which to employ them. In a word, as a man is said to have a right to his property, he may equally be said to have a property in his rights. (Levy, 1988, p. 267)

From this, we get a clear delineation of the origin of teacher tenure statutes that have been enacted by most states. Substantial due process must be involved if a school district wishes to take away this property right of a tenured teacher by denying him or her further employment. While many states have a *trial period* during which time a school district can evaluate the professional abilities of a teacher before making a decision on tenure, others have enacted legislation that effectively grants *instant tenure* upon hiring. It is obvious that the less time a school district has to make a tenure decision, the more cautious school leaders must be in their search procedures.

ENACTED FEDERAL POLICY

There is no argument that *students do not lose their constitutional rights when they enter the schoolhouse door.* However, it can be argued that some federal policies actually hinder the effectiveness of leadership in the daily operation of a school system. There are two glaring examples of federal policies that actually have had deleterious effects on a school leader's ability to operate a school system without unwarranted federal intrusion. These two federal policies, the Individuals with Disabilities Education Act (IDEA) and the No Child Left Behind Act (NCLB), have so dramatically altered the leadership landscape that they have become the proverbial *camel's nose under the tent* for school leaders.

IDEA was originally known as Public Law 94–142 (1972) and was titled the Education for All Handicapped Children Act (1992). It has borne its current title since it was reauthorized by Congress in 1992. When the original legislation was passed in 1972, it was part of a national movement to deinstitutionalize those who were previously believed to need custodial care, but not educational or other social services, for the remainder of their lives. The net effect was the infusion of thousands of children with handicapping conditions into a public school system that had heretofore not been held accountable for educating them. There is little argument that special needs students have accomplished more in terms of education and socialization than in the years prior to the passage of IDEA, but such gains have not come without cost to other school programs.

School districts are further challenged by IDEA due to the fact that health care professionals are becoming better at recognizing other forms of disabilities that affect a student's ability to learn in the same fashion, at the same rate, in the same environment as *regular education* students. When the original law was passed, the scope of services envisioned arguably included only two major categories of students: educable mentally retarded and trainable mentally retarded. In the early 21st century, however, other handicapping conditions, such as severe mental retardation; autism; attention deficit disorder and attention deficit hyperactivity disorder; speech, visual, and hearing deficiencies; and those who need physical and occupational therapy under both IDEA (1972) and Section 504 of the Americans with

Disabilities Act (1992), to mention but a few, are clamoring for services from the schools.

Two *bright line* cases in recent years have placed an even greater burden on local school districts to provide services to these students. A 1984 decision in a Texas case found that the school district must pay for a student's clean intermittent catheterization (CIC) under the Free and Appropriate Education aspects of IDEA (U.S. 883, 1984). In a more recent case, the school district was ordered to fund services providing CIC, suctioning of the student's tracheostomy, ventilator monitoring, and positioning in the wheelchair as part of the related services section of IDEA (U.S. 66, 1999). Previous court decisions had not held school districts financially liable for such extensive services.

Provision of services to handicapped students certainly seems like a good idea. When provided, those services allow the student to become a member of the school community and to be educated to his or her fullest potential. However, IDEA has had the effect of raising the rights of students in this program to the level of a federal entitlement. As such, IDEA students have a higher claim to education services than do students who are not eligible for this program. As a result, the monetary demands to meet the requirements of this program drain precious resources away from students who are not in this program. When the law was originally enacted in 1972, Congress set a goal of funding 40 percent of the costs of the program. To date, it has yet to fund even 10 percent of those costs. With increasing public resentment to higher taxes, even for public schools, the financial burden of services for IDEA students is becoming very troubling.

There are few school leaders who do not recognize and welcome the educational value of having handicapped students as part of the school setting. Problems arise, however, when IDEA students must be disciplined for infractions of school rules. One must ask, *Would there be differing discipline policies for regular education students as opposed to special needs students if the IDEA had not been en-*

acted in 1972? Regardless of the answer to this rhetorical question, the fact is that there is now a *double standard* when it comes to student discipline. Students who have documented Individual Education Plans (IEPs), as mandated under IDEA, must have any violation of school rules evaluated in terms of their handicapping condition. The basic question that must be answered for any such violation is the following: *Is the student's misbehavior (in terms of established school policy) a result of the student's handicapping condition?* Generally, if the answer is *yes*, the student cannot be suspended or expelled, and the student's placement in the educational program can only be changed through a change in the student's IEP.

Regardless of the benefit gained for the special needs student population with the onset of IDEA, it has created a double standard in many areas of program funding and student discipline for local school districts. When the discipline meted out to a student must be tempered by any causal factors arising out of his or her handicapping condition, parents of nonhandicapped students look askance at school leaders when their child is punished for the same violation of school rules.

The perfect storm may be on the horizon for the IDEA program as forces for various student advocacy groups coalesce into one. Parents of regular education students are demanding that more money be spent on their programs. Advocacy groups for handicapped children are equally vociferous about the need to maintain and increase services for that population. There is a growing disillusion among political leaders that the nation's educational system is not educating students to the *world-class* level that they would like to see attained. Without a change in federal policy, it is apparent that courts will increasingly side with parents seeking increased services for their handicapped students, which only further drains local coffers of precious resources for regular education students. Unless Congress finally addresses its stated obligation to *fully fund* the local costs of special needs students, a legal Armageddon is on the horizon.

Another federal policy that has recently stirred leadership to higher levels of activity is the enactment of the NCLB of 2001. Its basic tenets dictate that schools who are receiving Title I money must now hire teachers with higher levels of training, must annually test 95 percent of their students in mathematics and reading/language arts, must guarantee continuous progress toward a level of proficiency developed by the state, and must inform parents of students in low-performing schools of their right to transfer their children to other, high-performing schools, if they desire.

One of the main requirements of NCLB is to disaggregate testing data for various ethnic groups to force educators to make extra efforts to close the achievement gap between African American students and Hispanic students on one hand, and Caucasian and Asian students on the other. Another is the requirement that states adopt academic standards and produce test results that are comparable from year to year. This is called the *annual yearly progress* (AYP) facet of the law that has dire consequences for schools and staff members if AYP is not maintained over time.

Even schools that have a history of high performance on statewide assessments could have a problem with AYP if any of the demographic subgroups that the school is required to track do not make progress in meeting the state's objectives. If one group fails to make the required progress, it is assumed that the entire school is not making progress. Those schools that do not make AYP are subject to a full range of improvement measures and sanctions imposed by NCLB. Amendments in this area are certain to come.

In a time of teacher shortage, one of the more troubling aspects of NCLB for school leaders is the requirement involving staff selection and obligations for the local school district that is receiving Title I funding. The federal government, supposedly not interested by its charter (the Constitution) in education, now has established guidelines for what it calls *highly qualified* educators. In addition to teachers being required to hold a baccalaureate degree and state certification, newly hired elementary teachers must pass a *rigorous* state test demonstrating subject knowledge and teaching skills in reading, writing, mathematics, and other areas of the basic curriculum. Elementary teachers already employed must pass a test in each of the subject areas in which the teacher teaches or pass an evaluation based on a *high, objective, uniform state standard.*

Newly hired middle and secondary teachers who teach a *core* subject *any part* of the day must past a rigorous state academic subject test in each core subject that the teacher teaches, or must complete an academic major or a graduate degree or hold advanced certification in each of the core subjects. Current middle and secondary teachers who teach a core subject any part of the day must pass a rigorous state test in each core subject the teacher teaches, or must complete an academic major or graduate degree or hold advanced certification in each of the core subjects, or must pass an evaluation based on a high, objective, uniform state standard.

The new law also affects the hiring of teacher aides or paraprofessionals. This employee group must now have completed at least 48 college credits or hold an associate's or higher degree, or must have met a rigorous standard of quality and be able to demonstrate, through a formal state or local academic assessment, knowledge of and ability to assist in instruction.

School districts are required to ensure that all teachers covered by NCLB are highly qualified by the start of the 2005–2006 school year; ensure that minority and low-income students are not taught at higher rates than other students by unqualified, out-of-field, or inexperienced teachers; report the progress on the district and each school toward meeting measurable objectives; notify parents of children who are attending Title I schools of their right to know the professional qualifications of their child's teachers; and notify parents of their right to transfer their child to another school within the district.

While the new law has many detractors, it is doubtful that all states would be making exhaustive efforts toward high-stakes testing were it not for NCLB. Many states are also facing the issue of whether requiring students to pass a statewide assessment as a prerequisite to graduation is a policy matter for the state or for the local school district. In some states that have required that students pass a statewide assessment in order to graduate, a disproportionate number of minority and special needs students are being denied diplomas. Even though the students have achieved the local school district requirements, graduation is denied by the state. While NCLB has its detractors who decry the onus of high-stakes testing on teenage students, at least one recent study indicated that many minority students have benefited from the extra push mandated by the act (Viadero, 2003).

By far the most troublesome part of NCLB is that it calls for the removal of a school building's teachers and administrative leadership if AYP is not attained for four straight years. This will provide a most interesting legal question if this provision is ever enforced on a school building: Can the federal government, which explicitly acknowledges in the Tenth Amendment that it has no control over education in the states, actually disenfranchise teachers and school administrators at the local level for failure to meet an educational goal? You decide.

CONCLUSION

As you can see, the *giant umbrella* of laws, rules, and regulations under which a school leader must operate keeps expanding. The laws of the 50 states add greatly to the relatively few major items reviewed in this chapter. The true educational leader of the 21st century will take the time to become aware of the legal parameters under which he or she must operate. It takes more than a cursory course in school law. It takes constant attention to the legal landscape as it changes.

REFERENCES

Alexander, K., & Alexander, M. D. (2001). *American public school law* (5th ed.). Belmont, CA: Wadsworth/Thomson Learning.

Constitution of Virginia, the. (1971). Article I, 15.

Elementary and Secondary Education Act (ESEA) of 1965, reauthorized as No Child Left Behind Act of 2001, Pub. L. No. 107–110, 115 Stat. 1425 (2002).

Engel v. Vitale, 370 U.S. 421 (1962).

Green, E. B. (1941). *Religion and the state in America.* New York: New York University Press.

Individuals with Disabilities Education Act, Pub. L. No. 94–142 (1972).

Irving School District v. Tatro, 468 U.S. 883 (1984).

Lee v. Weisman, 505 U.S. 507 (1992).

Levy, W. L. (1988). *Original intent and the framers' constitution.* New York: Macmillan.

Mattocks, T. C. (2001). The aftermath of *Santa Fe v. Doe*: Is school prayer an option? *West's Education Law Reporter, 150*(2), 333–346.

Minersville School District v. Gobitis, 310 U.S. 586 (1940).

New Jersey v. TLO, 469 U.S. 325 (1985).

No Child Left Behind Act of 2001, Pub. L. No. 107–110, 115 Stat. 1425 (2002).

Rousseau, J. (1973). *A discourse on political economy* (G. D. H. Cole, Trans.). London: J. M. Dent and Sons. (Original work published 1758)

School District of Abington Township v. Schempp, 374 U.S. 203 (1963).

Tinker v. Des Moines Independent Community School District, 393 U.S. 503 (1969).

Viadero, D. (2003, April 16). Study finds higher gains in states with high-stakes tests. *Education Week,* p. 10.

West Virginia State Board of Education v. Barnette, 319 U.S. 624 (1943).

10

Leadership and Change: Lessons Learned from Great Companies and High-Performing Districts

E. E. (Gene) Davis

In the preceding chapters of this book, leadership knowledge, skills, and practices that are fundamental to any leadership position within the public schools were discussed. In this chapter, leadership is examined based on those themes but with a specific focus on leadership at the district level. The author contends that if reform activities are undertaken one classroom at a time, or even one school at a time, it will be a long time before student achievement reaches world-class standards in all of the more than 14,000 school districts across the country.

Furthermore, the kind of leadership that is to be found in high-performing school districts and great companies is also addressed. Previously, the focus of research on leadership has been primarily on the school level. Recent research has begun to look at the district as the focal point for leading change and achieving high performance. Similarly, leadership in the private sector has focused on the leadership of great companies (Collins, 2001, Kouzes & Posner, 2002). This chapter is designed to bring it all together regarding the leadership that is necessary to bring about success for all schools.

LEADERSHIP AT THE DISTRICT LEVEL: THEN AND NOW

The research on leadership for school improvement over the past 30 years has *spotlighted* the role of the building principal. While the research is compelling, the environment within which a school principal operated in the past was much different than it is today. The movement to *site-based* management in the late 1980s and early 1990s enhanced the view that improved education—student achievement—would happen only if schools were in charge of their own destiny. This view was further reinforced with the increased involvement of state and federal policy bodies with reforms in the 1980s that essentially created a *backseat role* for the superintendent and local boards (Glass, Bjork, & Brunner, 2000).

However, in the 1990s most states had either adopted standards for instruction linked to state assessments or were well on their way to doing so. The result was the realization that the superintendent could no longer simply *manage* the district and *delegate* school improvement to the schools but must assume a greater leadership role with improving student achievement. Togneri and Anderson (2003), in a report for the Learning First Alliance, said it best:

> Heroic principals who turn around low-performing schools, innovative charter schools that break established molds, inspiring teachers who motivate students to excel—those are the familiar prescriptions for improving student achievement in high-poverty schools. While such efforts may mean brighter educational futures for the children involved, they produce isolated islands of excellence. (p. 1)

Further, the Learning First Alliance called for "policymakers, practitioners, and the public to accept the challenge of improving student achievement across entire school systems" (Togneri & Anderson, 2003, p. 1).

Given the current era of accountability as evidenced not only by the standards-based environment but also more recently by the passage by Congress of the No Child Left Behind Act (2002), what is the role of the leader of a school district—generally referred to as the superintendent? Further, what leadership lessons are available that can guide the leaders of our nation's school systems in this period of substantial change? Clearly the responsibility for improved student achievement has shifted from the school-building level to the district office. While each principal continues to be accountable for student achievement in his or her building, the multiple measures for making progress toward achieving proscribed standards requirements for employing *highly qualified* teachers and for public reporting of the progress made in schools and districts, as outlined in both state and federal legislation, necessitates a systematic, districtwide approach.

Fortunately, recent books, reports, studies, and dissertations are increasingly addressing the leadership knowledge, skills, and practices that are essential to the leadership of school systems. In addition, research on leadership of successful private companies is providing guidance to those who seek information about leading districtwide change. One book in particular, *Good to Great: Why Some Companies Make the Leap . . . and Others Don't* by Jim Collins (2001), should be especially beneficial to those who are current or aspiring superintendents.

An essential ingredient to achieving the leadership mind-set in the current accountability environment is for leaders of districts to think differently about their roles. Carter and Cunningham (1997, p. 242) note that as superintendents, "we have an opportunity to reinvent ourselves. But what do we want to be?"

Expectations of superintendent leadership have generally focused on what has been known as the 4 Bs: buses, budgets, buildings, and behavior. In fact, Oxford's dictionary defines "superintend" as "manage, watch, and direct" (work, etc.), and "superintendent" as "one who superintends—director of institution, etc., police officer above the rank of inspector" (Allen, 1984). Unfortunately, the view of most state legislative bodies, local school boards, and district employees toward superintendent leadership has mirrored *Oxford*'s definition.

Until recently, job vacancy announcements for the superintendency emphasized the need for candidates to possess skills in fiscal management, facility operation and maintenance, good communication, school law, and, in some instances, a good sense of humor. The areas that are critical for today's district leaders, such as curriculum, instruction, and assessment, were rarely if ever mentioned. Obviously, some school districts have been ahead of the curve, but for the most part, the previous description of the leadership role for superintendents was centered on management tasks.

An example of how district employees view the leadership role of the superintendent is best described by one building principal, who while conversing with the superintendent, who had visited the school on numerous occasions during the school year, said, "Why are you always in the schools? Don't you have superintendent things to do?" (Davis, 1990).

Given the magnitude of the research on principal leadership as the key to effective school reform, it is not surprising that the aforementioned principal believed that the superintendent's leadership would not have an impact in his school. While that may have been the case in the 1980s and early 1990s, it is certainly not the case now. The era of accountability for *all* students to learn at a high level has refocused the leadership spotlight to the district level.

LEADERSHIP LESSONS FROM GREAT COMPANIES AND HIGH-PERFORMING SCHOOL DISTRICTS

The leadership of the superintendent of schools is becoming the single most important factor in assuring that district-wide expectations and structures are in place that result in high academic achievement for all students. Recent research by Cawelti and Protheroe (2003), Ragland, Asera, and Johnson (as cited in Cawelti & Protheroe, 2003); Chrispeels (2002), Togneri and Anderson (2003), Cawelti and Protheroe (2003), and Hoyle, Bjork, Collier, and Glass (2004) are examples of only a few of the more well-known studies. In addition, Collins (2001) refers to "Level 5 Leadership" characteristics that result in companies becoming great:

- First Who . . . Then What
- Confront the Brutal Facts
- Hedgehog Concept
- Culture of Discipline
- Technology Accelerators

Collins clearly delineates how Level 5 Leadership translates into results. Are there similarities between the leadership of great companies and high-performing school districts? Absolutely! Is there a one-to-one match between the two situations? No. But there is sufficient similarity to strongly suggest that current and future district leaders and superintendents should look seriously at the research; less with the thought that, "Well, you can't do that as a superintendent," and more to thinking more broadly about what both private and public sector research says about leading effective organizations.

While the language used to provide evidence of the similarities between leaders and leadership practices in great companies and high-performing school districts may be different, the results will be the same. Perhaps the best way to analyze the leadership tenets noted earlier is to provide a table; readers can draw their own conclusions from the information in table 10.1.

The characteristics of good to great companies and high-performing districts reported here are markedly similar. Unquestionably, the superintendent of a school district may encounter more difficulty achieving all nine of the characteristics than the CEO of a private company. Two examples are noted here:

- Superintendents typically *inherit* personnel deeply embedded in the community—particularly in rural and small communities—making it difficult to achieve the "First who . . . then what" (Collins, 2001) characteristic of great companies. CEOs usually have greater authority in the selection of key personnel, in many instances bringing key people with them when they assume leadership of a company.

Table 10.1. Characteristics of Good to Great Companies and High-Performing School Districts

Great Companies	High-Performing School Districts
"Level 5 Leadership"—Leaders channel their ego needs away from themselves and into the larger goals of building a great company (p. 21).	"Superintendents established a clear and powerful role in communicating the message that high student achievement was a responsibility shared by everyone in the district" (Ragland, Asera, & Johnson, 1999, p. 11).
First Who, Then What—Leaders first "get the right people on the bus, the wrong people off the bus, and the right people in the right seats" (p. 13).	Superintendents in high-performing school districts restructure and/or redefine the roles of the district office personnel (Cawelti & Protheroe, 2001, p. 15; Togneri & Anderson, 2003, p. 7).
Confront the Brutal Facts—(Yet Never Lose Faith) (p. 13)	"Let truth be heard." High-performing districts are willing to acknowledge student achievement did not meet expectations, and to forthrightly address the problem (Togneri & Anderson, 2003, p. 49).
"The Hedgehog Concept, Simplicity Within the Three Circles—What you can be the best in the world at, what drives your economic engine, and what are you deeply passionate about" (pp. 13, 95–96).	"Districts instilled visions that focused on student learning and guided instructional improvement" (Togneri & Anderson, 2003, p. 6). "Districts committed to sustaining reform over the long haul" (Togneri & Anderson, 2003, p. 8); Districts addressed issues of teachers feeling overwhelmed: "If we can reach consensus, we'll take some things out of the curriculum" (Cawelti & Protheroe, 2001, p. 57). High-performing districts had "constant and consistent professional development" (North Carolina Department of Education, 2000, p. 6).
A Culture of Discipline—All companies have a culture, some companies have discipline, but few companies have a culture of discipline (Collins, 2001).	"Working together takes work" (Togneri & Anderson, 2003, p. 50). Collaboration for common goals required avoiding enmity, careful selection of tools to ensure a focus on students and

learning, and adopting a mentality that there are no quick fixes. In the final analysis, high-performing districts assured that leadership was expected and shared across the system.

Superintendents reduced "distractions that would otherwise divert the energy of principals and teachers . . . and continuously focused staff attention and energies on instruction" (Ragland et al., 1999, p. 15).

Another Note: A practical example is to reconsider each state or federal funding opportunity in relation to the strategic goal of improving learning. This is in contrast to the general approach of applying for any and all grants primarily to gain some fiscal resources to replace those lost through budget reduction. One approach continues the focus on the primary mission of the district, and the other focuses almost entirely on securing additional resources even though the district may need to change direction if they are funded. Collins (2001) addresses this through his discussion of the "stop-doing list" (p. 139).

High-Performing Districts: "Exhibit applications of computer technology connected to instructional programs. . . . Although one segment of the literature on technology applications for education stridently asserts that it will change the landscape of American schools, a more thoughtful group acknowledge that it provides a powerful tool for improving learning and teaching." (Hoyle et al., 2004).

(*continued*)

"The good to great companies used technology as an accelerator of momentum, not a creator of it" (p. 112).

Table 10.1. *(Continued)*

Great Companies	High-Performing School Districts
"The good to great companies understood a simple truth—tremendous power exists in the fact of continuous improvement and the delivery of results" (p. 174).	High-performing districts committed to sustaining reform over the long haul (Togneri & Anderson, 2003, p. 8).
Key words for long term success are consistency and coherence (Collins, 2001)—"Each piece of the system reinforces the other parts of the system to form an integrated whole that is much more powerful than the sum of the parts" (p. 182).	"The districts in this category understand that making a difference takes time. They set their courses and stayed with them for years. They also experienced remarkable stability in their leadership" (Togneri & Anderson, 2003, p. 8).
"In a good to great transformation, budgeting is a discipline to decide which arenas *should be fully funded and which should not be funded at all*" (p. 140).	Avoidance of a heavy reliance on "short-term funding" (Togneri & Anderson, 2003, p. 50). Reallocating fiscal resources to address critical priorities tied to improved student learning is critical to long-term success. Decisions regarding what not to continue doing become as important as what to do.

Source: All citations under "Great Companies" are from Collins (2001).

- Superintendents must meet regularly with publicly elected board members—sometimes more than once each month—for authorization of proposed change activities, expenditure of budget funds, employment, transfer and/or termination of personnel, and most major direction changes planned for the organization. CEOs usually meet with their board and stockholders on an annual basis.

Other examples could be provided, but the aforementioned ones exemplify the major differences between the superintendent of a school district and the CEO of a company. However, these examples of difficulties experienced by superintendents do not negate the significance of the similarities between what CEOs of great companies do and what superintendents of high-performing districts do to achieve expected results. Obviously, superintendents will have to work within the boundaries of state laws, local history, and practice, but it is also obvious that several superintendents have been able to do this quite successfully (Cawelti & Protheroe, 2003).

IMPLICATIONS FOR SUPERINTENDENTS

What are the practical implications for the research on great companies and high-performing school districts? What steps would a superintendent need to take in order to begin the process of achieving high-performing status?

Chrispeels (2002) in an article in the *Journal for Effective Schools* describes the Effective Schools Process as a framework for achieving district change leading to high-performance results. Many of the steps of the Effective Schools Process mirror the characteristics of great companies and high-performing districts. Figure 10.1 identifies the details of this process.

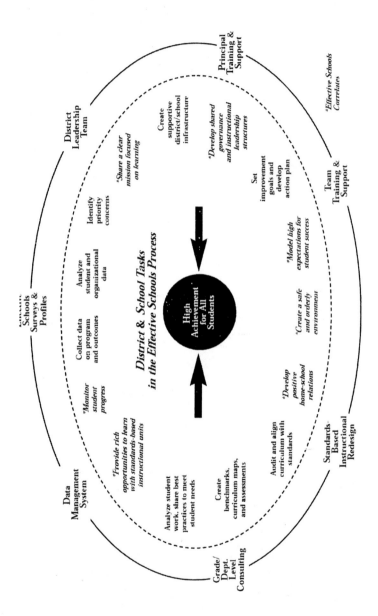

Figure 10.1. Model of a districtwide Effective Schools Reform Process showing services provided by the California Center for Effective Schools and tasks undertaken by the district and schools to bring about change. The figure was taken from the article by Chrispeels in the *Journal for Effective Schools*.

A review of figure 10.1 indicates several matches with the characteristics of great companies and high-performing districts. Some matches are the following:

- Establish a district leadership team.
- Share a clear mission focused on student learning.
- Provide principal training.
- Collect data on programs and outcomes.
- Analyze student and organizational data.
- Create benchmarks and assessments.
- Develop positive home-school relations.
- Model expectations for student success.
- Identify priority concerns.

The implication is clear—CEOs of great companies and superintendents of high-performing school districts define a *framework* within which expected results will be achieved and marshal both the human and fiscal resources necessary to achieve the desired ends. Leadership in their organization does not *just happen*. Purposeful activities are undertaken that become *a way of doing business* as opposed to the most recent *fad* or *silver bullet* approach practiced by organizations that do not meet the exemplary level of performance.

What steps should current and aspiring superintendents take to move toward high-performing status?

1. Recognize and understand the research on great companies and high-performing districts.
2. Adopt a research-based framework that mirrors item 1, above, understanding that flexibility is critical. The Effective Schools Process is one framework that has proven successful in high-performing districts.
3. Prepare local boards, staff, and communities for the organizational governance changes necessary to reach the level of high performance.

4. Redefine and/or restructure the organization based on the tenets of great companies and high-performing districts.
5. Provide consistent and congruent development opportunities for all key personnel.
6. Work diligently to get the *right people on the bus* and the *wrong people off.*
7. Redefine the budgeting and funding processes to focus available resources on the most critical priorities.
8. Recognize that the focus must be on the long term; rethink the traditional career path, for example, move every 3 years to a bigger and supposedly better job.
9. Insist that university administrator preparation programs include research and practices of great companies and high-performing districts in their programs.
10. Recognize that one person cannot accomplish the expected results. The *lone ranger* no longer exists in this environment.

Finally, note that the majority of the chapters in this book are in many ways related to the characteristics of great companies and high-performing districts. Leadership in both types of organizations requires a rethinking and in a majority of instances a reinventing of the leader's beliefs and practices. It also requires a reexamination of the influence that the superintendent of schools has on school district improvement.

REFERENCES

Allen, R. E. (Ed.). (1984). *The pocket Oxford dictionary of current English.* New York: Clarendon.

Carter, G. R., & Cunningham, W. G. (1997). *The American school superintendent: Leading in an age of pressure.* San Francisco: Jossey-Bass.

Cawelti, G., & Protheroe, N. (2003). *Supporting school improvement: Lessons from districts successfully meeting the challenge.* Arlington, VA: Educational Research Service.

Chrispeels, J. H. (2002). An emerging conceptual and practical framework for implementing districtwide effective schools reform. *Journal for Effective Schools, 1*(1), 17–30.

Collins, J. (2001). *Good to great: Why some companies make the leap . . . and others don't.* New York: HarperCollins.

Davis, E. E. (1990). Personal communication.

Glass, T. E., Bjork, L., & Brunner, C. C. (2000). *The study of the American school superintendency—2000: A look at the superintendent of education in the new millennium.* Arlington, VA: American Association of School Administrators.

Hoyle, J., Bjork, L., Collier, V., & Glass, T. (2004). *The superintendent as CEO: Standards-based performance.* Thousand Oaks, CA: Corwin.

Kouzes, J. M., & Posner, B. Z. (2002). *Leadership the challenge* (2nd ed.). San Francisco: Jossey-Bass.

No Child Left Behind Act of 2001, Pub. L. No. 107–110, 115 Stat. 1425 (2002).

Ragland, M. A., Asera, R., & Johnson, J. F., Jr. (1999). *Urgency, responsibility, and efficacy: Preliminary findings of a study of high-performing Texas school districts.* Austin, TX: The Charles A. Dana Center, The University of Texas at Austin.

Togneri, W., & Anderson, S. E. (2003). *Beyond islands of excellence: What districts can do to improve instruction and achievement in schools.* Washington, DC: Learning First Alliance.

Index

About the Contributors

E. E. (Gene) Davis is director of the Intermountain Center for Education Effectiveness and professor and chair of the education leadership department at Idaho State University. Prior to joining Idaho State University, Dr. Davis was a superintendent of two large, rapidly growing school districts for 10 years. He has worked as a teacher, principal, and assistant superintendent during his 42-year career. He has been recognized as an Executive Educator 100 and has received the American Association of School Administrators (AASA) Leadership for Learning Award; the NEA School Bell Award; the ACT-SO award from the NAACP; Gold Medallion Award from the National School Publications Association; the Eaton Award, the highest award given for excellence in Idaho economic education; and the United Way Gold Award. He has served as executive-in-residence at Virginia Commonwealth University, Richmond, Virginia; an education representative to Japan for the Japanese Foundation, Tokyo; and an education representative to Germany for Phillip Morris, USA and Korber International, Rhinebeck, Germany. Dr. Davis is executive editor of the *Journal for Effective Schools*, has published more than 80 technical and evaluation reports for schools across the United States, has served as a trainer for the United States Air University, and has written numerous articles. He has coauthored, with Dr. M. Donald Thomas, two Phi Delta Kappa Education Foundation fastbacks: *Legal and Ethical Basis for Educational Leadership* and *An Adequate Education Defined*. Dr. Davis received his Ed.D. from the University of Montana.

William L. Bainbridge currently serves as president and CEO of SchoolMatch and as a Distinguished Research Professor at the University of Dayton, Ohio. He is the former superintendent of three school districts in Ohio and Virginia and former assistant to the Ohio Superintendent of Public Instruction. He was named Educator of the Year by the Ohio PTA and has served as educational consultant to more than 400 corporations and hundreds of school systems. He has been a fellow of the American College of Forensic Examiners and Diplomate of the National Academy for School Executives. He has appeared on NBC's *Today Show*, ABC's *Good Morning America*, CNN, NPR, CBS radio, and more than 400 national and local television and radio programs. He earned his Ph.D. in education and business at Ohio State University and has since completed executive education at Columbia University, the National Academy for School Executives, the Fisher College of Business at Ohio State University, and the Disney Institute.

Dale L. Brubaker is a professor of educational leadership and cultural studies at the University of North Carolina at Greensboro. He was an assistant professor at the University of California, Santa Barbara, and an associate professor at the University of Wisconsin, Milwaukee. He is the author or coauthor of more than 20 books, including *Alternative Directions for the Social Studies, Social Studies in a Mass Society, Creative Survival in Educational Bureaucracies, Creative Curriculum Leadership, Staying on Track, Theses and Dissertations,* and *Avoiding Thesis and Dissertation Pitfalls*. He holds a B.A. from Albion College, and a M.Ed. and Ph.D. from Michigan State University.

Ross Danis is a program officer for the Geraldine R. Dodge Foundation. Prior to joining the Dodge Foundation, Dr. Danis worked at all levels in the New Jersey public school education system, most recently as the assistant superintendent of the Randolph Township School District. He has worked as a staff developer for the Academy for the Advancement of Teaching and Management. A past president of the board of trustees of the Principals' Center for the Garden State, he currently holds tenure as a charter member. As a Dodge Fellow, he was the subject of a documentary on the principalship titled *Quicksand and Banana Peels: A Year in the Life of Two Principals*. Coauthor of a number of articles and papers, he currently teaches a doctoral-level course on leadership at Seton Hall University, East Orange, New Jersey, and continues to write and present courses and workshops on a variety of educational and organizational topics. Dr. Danis earned an Ed.D. in educational leadership from Nova Southeastern University.

Karen M. Dyer is the manager of the education sector for the Center for Creative Leadership in Greensboro, North Carolina. She was formerly the executive director of the Chicago Academy for School Leadership. Dr. Dyer has served as the executive director of the Bay Area and North Bay School Leadership Centers, both part of the California School Leadership Academy. Dr. Dyer has made presentations for the ASCD, NSDC, NAESP, NSBA, NBPTS, the College of William and Mary, and the comprehensive school reform program, Co-nect. She has done consultation work with school districts in Alaska, California, Illinois, Maryland, Mississippi, North Carolina, and Virginia. Dr. Dyer is the coauthor of the book *The Intuitive Principal: A Guide to Leadership* and numerous instructional leadership modules, including *Principally Speaking: What Principals Need to Know About the National Board for Professional Teaching Standards*. Dr. Dyer holds a doctorate in education administration from the University of the Pacific in Stockton, California.

Donald C. Lueder is a professor of educational leadership in the Department of Counseling and Leadership in the College of Education at Winthrop University in Rock Hill, South Carolina. During his tenure at Winthrop, Dr. Lueder has served as chair of the department and dean of the college. Before joining the faculty at Winthrop, Dr. Lueder was the director of the Center of Excellence for the Study of

Disadvantaged Children and Basic Skill Development at Tennessee State University in Nashville. Dr. Lueder has served as a professor of educational leadership at Peabody College of Vanderbilt University, Tennessee State University in Nashville, and the University of North Carolina at Charlotte. In addition, he has been a high school teacher, principal, and central office administrator.

T. C. "Chris" Mattocks has served as a local school district superintendent for more than 25 years. He is currently superintendent of the Bellingham, Massachusetts, school district. He has previously been superintendent of two school districts in Idaho (Rexburg and Idaho Falls) and was a superintendent in three Montana school districts (Custer, Fairview, and Cut Bank) prior to his service in Idaho. He also served as assistant dean of the College of Education and associate professor of education law at Idaho State University from 1996–2002. He received his Ed.D. from Montana State University.

M. Donald Thomas is a former superintendent of the Salt Lake City School District (1973–1984) and deputy superintendent for South Carolina (1984–1987). He is the recipient of the NAACP Civil Rights Worker of the Year Award, the American Association of School Administrators (AASA) Distinguished Service Award, the Horace Mann League Educator of the Year Award (1997), and the Don Quixote Award for services to special needs children. Thomas previously served as senior national faculty for Nova Southeastern University's national Ed.D. program for educational leaders and as a director for the Network for Effective Schools. He has published extensively and is the author of six Phi Delta Kappa fastbacks. He earned his doctorate at the University of Illinois and did postdoctoral work at Stanford University.

Date Due
